"My trust in God's Word is greater, my submission to God's Word is deeper, and my love for God's Word is sweeter as a result of reading this book. For these reasons, I cannot recommend it highly enough."

David Platt, Senior Pastor, The Church at Brook Hills,
Birmingham, Alabama; author, *Radical: Taking Back Your Faith from the American Dream*

"This little book is a highly readable introduction to Scripture's teaching about Scripture that preserves the contours of a responsible and informed doctrine of Scripture, without getting bogged down in arcane details. Buy this book by the case and distribute copies to elders, deacons, Sunday school teachers, and anyone in the church who wants to understand a little better what the Bible is. Bad doctrine springs in part from ignorance. Blessed are those teachers and preachers in the church who, like the author of this book, combat ignorance by getting across mature theology in a lucid style that avoids generating theological indigestion."

D. A. Carson, Research Professor of New Testament,
Trinity Evangelical Divinity School

"One of my prayers for the next twenty years of ministry, if the Lord sees fit to grant me that, is that we might see the level of biblical literacy exponentially grow. For that to happen we must learn what the Scriptures are and how heavily we can lean on them. Kevin DeYoung serves this end well in *Taking God At His Word*. May the God of the Word be known and cherished all the more because of this little book."

Matt Chandler, Lead Pastor, The Village Church, Dallas, Texas;
President, Acts 29 Church Planting Network

"This is a brilliant, succinct, yet thorough study of the authority and sufficiency of Scripture, based on what Scripture says about itself. Clarity and passion are the distinguishing marks of Kevin DeYoung's writing, and this may be his finest, most important work yet."

John MacArthur, Pastor, Grace Community Church,
Sun Valley, California

"If you're looking for a clearly and simply stated doctrine of Scripture, here it is. Kevin DeYoung has accomplished his aim of communicating what the Bible says about the Bible. He's done it with the qualities we have come to anticipate from him: efficiency, pastoral care, wit, and rigor. Most of all, he has let the Word speak for itself."

Kathleen B. Nielson, Director of Women's Initiatives,
The Gospel Coalition

Taking God At His Word

Taking God At His Word

WHY THE BIBLE IS KNOWABLE,
NECESSARY, AND ENOUGH, AND
WHAT THAT MEANS FOR YOU AND ME

KEVIN DeYOUNG

CROSSWAY

WHEATON, ILLINOIS

Hardcover ISBN: 978-1-4335-4240-4
ePub ISBN: 978-1-4335-4243-5
PDF ISBN: 978-1-4335-4241-1
Mobipocket ISBN: 978-1-4335-4242-8

Library of Congress Cataloging-in-Publication Data
DeYoung, Kevin.
   Taking God at his word : why the Bible is knowable,
necessary, and enough, and what that
means for you and me / Kevin DeYoung.
     pages cm
   Includes bibliographical references and index.
   ISBN 978-1-4335-4240-4 (hc)
   1. Bible—Evidences, authority, etc. 2. Bible—Inspiration.
I. Title.
BS480.D49   2014
220.1—dc23   2013040668

Crossway is a publishing ministry of Good News Publishers.

LB		24	23	22	21	20	19	18	17	16	15	14
15	14	13	12	11	10	9	8	7	6	5	4	3	2	1

To the saints who are in East Lansing,
for listening to a decade's worth of sermons
and always taking God at his Word

Contents

1

Believing,
Feeling, Doing

My soul keeps your testimonies; I love them exceedingly.

PSALM 119:167

This book begins in a surprising place: with a love poem.

Don't worry, it's not from me. It's not from my wife. It's not from a card, a movie, or the latest power ballad. It's not a new poem or a short poem. But it is most definitely a love poem. You may have read it before. You may have sung it, too. It's the longest chapter in the longest book in the longest half of a very long collection of books. Out of 1,189 chapters scattered across 66 books written over the course of two millennia, Psalm 119 is the longest.[1]

And for good reason.

This particular psalm is an acrostic. There are 8 verses in each stanza, and within each stanza the 8 verses begin with the same letter of the Hebrew alphabet. So verses 1–8 all begin with *aleph*, verses 9–16 with *beth*, verses 17–24 with

[1] Psalm 119 is the longest chapter in the Bible by any definition (if we care to look at chapters, which, we should remember, aren't inspired divisions). Determining the longest book of the Bible is a little trickier. Psalms is the longest book of the Bible if you count chapters or verses. It also takes up the most pages in our English Bibles. But since chapters, verses, and page numbers are not a part of the original manuscripts, scholars have come up with other ways to determine the length of an individual book. Depending on the means of calculation, Jeremiah, Genesis, and Ezekiel may be longer than Psalms.

gimel, and on and on for 22 stanzas and 176 verses—all of them exultant in their love for God's word. In 169 of these verses, the psalmist makes some reference to the word of God. Law, testimonies, precepts, statutes, commandments, rules, promises, word—this language appears in almost every verse, and often more than once in the same verse. The terms have different shades of meaning (e.g., what God wants, or what God appoints, or what God demands, or what God has spoken), but they all center on the same big idea: God's revelation in words.

Surely it is significant that this intricate, finely crafted, single-minded love poem—the longest in the Bible—is not about marriage or children or food or drink or mountains or sunsets or rivers or oceans, but about the Bible itself.

The Poet's Passion

I imagine many of us dabbled in poetry way back when. You know, years before you had kids, before you got engaged, or, if you're young enough, before last semester. I've written a few poems in my day, and even if we were best friends I still wouldn't show them to you. I'm not embarrassed by the subject matter—writing for and about my lovely bride—but I doubt the form is anything to be proud of. For most of us, writing a love poem is like making cookies with wheat germ—it's supposed to be the real thing but doesn't taste quite right.

Some love poems are amazing, like Shakespeare's Sonnet 116: "Let me not to the marriage of true minds admit impediments. Love is not love which alters when it alteration finds," and all that jazz. Beautiful. Brilliant. Breathtaking.

Other poems, not so much. Like this poem I found online by a man reliving his teenage romantic genius:

Look! There's a lonely cow
Hay! Cow!
If I were a cow, that would be me
If love is the ocean, I'm the Titanic.
Baby I burned my hand on
The frying pan of our love
But still it feels better
Than the bubble gum that hold us together
Which you stepped on

Words fail, don't they? Both in commenting on the poem and in the poem itself. Still, this bovine- and bubble gum–themed piece of verbal art does more with subtlety and imagery than the entry entitled "Purse of Love":

Girl you make me
Brush my teeth
Comb my hair
Use deodorant
Call you
You're so swell

I suppose this poem may capture a moment of real sacrifice for our high school hero. But whatever the earnestness of intention, it is strikingly bad poetry. Most poems written when we are young and in love feel, in retrospect—how shall we say?—a bit awkward. This is partly because few teenagers are instinctively good poets. It's about as common as cats being instinctively friendly. But the other reason our old love poems can be painful to read is that we find ourselves uncomfortable with the exuberant passion and extravagant praise. We think, "Yikes! I sound like a nineteen-year-old in love. I can't believe I was so over-the-top. Talk about melo-dramatic!" It can be embarrassing to get reacquainted with our earlier unbounded enthusiasm and unbridled affection, especially if the relationship being praised never worked out or if the love has since grown cold.

I wonder if we read a poem like Psalm 119 and feel a bit of the same embarrassment. I mean, look at verses 129–136, for example:

Your testimonies are wonderful;
> therefore my soul keeps them.

The unfolding of your words gives light;
> it imparts understanding to the simple.

I open my mouth and pant,
> because I long for your commandments.

Turn to me and be gracious to me,
> as is your way with those who love your name.

Keep steady my steps according to your promise,
> and let no iniquity get dominion over me.

Redeem me from man's oppression,
> that I may keep your precepts.

Make your face shine upon your servant,
> and teach me your statutes.

My eyes shed streams of tears,
> because people do not keep your law.

This is pretty emotional stuff—panting, longing, weeping streams of tears. If we're honest, it sounds like high school love poetry on steroids. It's passionate and sincere, but a little unrealistic, a little too dramatic for real life. Who actually feels this way about commandments and statutes?

Finishing at the Start

I can think of three different reactions to the long, repetitive passion for the word of God in Psalm 119.

The first reaction is, "Yeah, right." This is the attitude of the skeptic, the scoffer, and the cynic. You think to yourself, "It's nice that ancient people had such respect for God's laws and God's words, but we can't take these things too seriously. We know that humans often put words in God's mouth for their own purposes. We know that every 'divine' word is mixed with human thinking, redaction, and interpretation. The Bible, as we have it, is inspiring in parts, but it's also antiquated, indecipherable at times, and frankly, incorrect in many places."

The second reaction is "Ho, hum." You don't have any particular problems with honoring God's word or believing the Bible. On paper, you have a high view of the Scriptures. But in practice, you find them tedious and usually irrelevant. You think to yourself, though never voicing this out loud, "Psalm 119 is too long. It's boring. It's the worst day in my Bible reading plan. The thing goes on forever and ever saying the same thing. I like Psalm 23 much better."

If the first reaction is "Yeah, right" and the second reaction is "Ho, hum," the third possible reaction is "Yes! Yes! Yes!" This is what you cry out when everything in Psalm 119 rings true in your head and resonates in your heart, when the psalmist perfectly captures your passions, your affections, and your actions (or at least what you want them to be). This is when you think to yourself, "I love this psalm because it gives voice to the song in my soul."

The purpose of this book is to get us to fully, sincerely, and consistently embrace this third response. I want all that is in Psalm 119 to be an expression of all that is in our heads and in our hearts. In effect, I'm starting this book with the conclusion. Psalm 119 is the goal. I want to convince you (and make sure I'm convinced myself) that the Bible makes no mistakes, can be understood, cannot be overturned, and is the most important word in your life, the most relevant thing you can read each day. Only when we are convinced of all this can we give a full-throated "Yes! Yes! Yes!" every time we read the Bible's longest chapter.

Think of this chapter as application and the remaining seven chapters of this book as the necessary building blocks so that the conclusions of Psalm 119 are warranted. Or, if I can use a more memorable metaphor, think of chapters 2 through 8 as seven different vials poured into a bubbling cauldron and this chapter as the catalytic result. Psalm 119 shows us what to believe about the word of God, what to feel about the word of God, and what to do with the word of God. That's the application. That's the chemical reaction produced in God's people when we pour into our heads and hearts the sufficiency of Scripture, the authority of Scripture, the clarity of Scripture, and everything else we will encounter in the remaining seven chapters. Psalm 119 is the explosion of praise made possible by an orthodox and evangelical doctrine of Scripture. When we embrace everything the Bible says about itself, then—and only then—will we believe what we should believe about the word of God, feel what we should feel, and do with the word of God what we ought to do.

What Should I Believe about the Word of God?

In Psalm 119 we see at least three essential, irreducible characteristics we should believe about God's word.

First, God's word says what is true. Like the psalmist, we can trust in the word (v. 42), knowing that it is altogether true (v. 142). We can't trust everything we read on the Internet. We can't trust everything we hear from our professors. We certainly can't trust all the facts given by our politicians. We can't even trust the fact-checkers who check those facts! Statistics can be manipulated. Photographs can be faked. Magazine covers can be airbrushed. Our teachers, our friends, our science, our studies, even our eyes can deceive us. But the word of God is entirely true and always true:

- God's word is firmly fixed in the heavens (v. 89); it doesn't change.
- There is no limit to its perfection (v. 96); it contains nothing corrupt.
- All God's righteous rules endure forever (v. 160); they never get old and never wear out.

If you ever think to yourself, "I need to know what is true—what is true about me, true about people, true about the world, true about the future, true about the past, true about the good life, and true about God," then come to God's word. It teaches only what is true: "Sanctify them in the truth," Jesus said; "your word is truth" (John 17:17).

Second, God's word demands what is right. The psalmist gladly acknowledges God's right to issue commands and humbly accepts that all these commands are right. "I know, O LORD, that your rules are righteous," he says (Ps. 119:75).

All God's commandments are sure (v. 86). All his precepts are right (v. 128). I sometimes hear Christians admit that they don't like what the Bible says, but since it's the Bible they have to obey it. On one level, this is an admirable example of submitting oneself to the word of God. And yet, we should go one step further and learn to see the goodness and rightness in all that God commands. We should love what God loves and delight in whatever he says. God does not lay down arbitrary rules. He does not give orders so that we might be restricted and miserable. He never requires what is impure, unloving, or unwise. His demands are always noble, always just, and always righteous.

Third, God's word provides what is good. According to Psalm 119, the word of God is the way of happiness (vv. 1–2), the way to avoid shame (v. 6), the way of safety (v. 9), and the way of good counsel (v. 24). The word gives us strength (v. 28) and hope (v. 43). It provides wisdom (vv. 98–100, 130) and shows us the way we should go (v. 105). God's verbal revelation, whether in spoken form in redemptive history or in the covenantal documents of redemptive history (i.e., the Bible), is unfailingly perfect. As the people of God, we believe the word of God can be trusted in every way to speak what is true, command what is right, and provide us with what is good.

What Should I Feel about the Word of God?

Too often, Christians reflect on only what they should believe about the word of God. But Psalm 119 will not let us stop there. This love poem forces us to consider how we feel about the word of God. We see that the psalmist has three fundamental affections for God's word.

First, he delights in it. Testimonies, commandments, law—they are all his delight (vv. 14, 24, 47, 70, 77, 143, 174). The psalmist can't help but speak of God's word in the deepest emotive language. The words of Scripture are sweet like honey (v. 103), the joy of his heart (v. 111), and positively wonderful (v. 129). "My soul keeps your testimonies," writes the psalmist; "I love them exceedingly" (v. 167).

But some people say, "I will never love the word of God like this. I'm not an intellectual. I don't listen to sermons all day. I don't read all the time. I'm not the sort of person who delights in words." That may be true as a general rule, but I'll bet there are times you get passionate about words on a page. We all pay attention when the words we are hearing or reading are of great benefit to us, like a will or an acceptance letter. We can read carefully when the text before us warns of great danger, like instructions on an electrical panel. We delight to read stories about us and about those we love. We love to read about greatness, beauty, and power. Do you see how I've just described the Bible? It's a book with great benefit to us, and one with grave warnings. It is a book about us and those we love. And most of all, it's a book that brings us face-to-face with One who possesses all greatness, beauty, and power. To be sure, the Bible can feel dull at times, but taken as a whole it is the greatest story ever told, and those who know it best are usually those who delight in it most.

Over and over, the psalmist professes his great love for the commands and testimonies of God (vv. 48, 97, 119, 127, 140).The flip side of this love is the anger he experiences when God's word is not delighted in. Hot indignation seizes him because of the wicked, who forsake God's law (v. 53). Zeal consumes him when his foes forget God's words (v. 139).

The faithless and disobedient he looks upon with disgust (v. 158). The language may sound harsh to us, but that's an indication of how little we treasure the word of God. How do you feel when someone fails to see the beauty you see in your spouse? Or when people don't see what makes your special-needs child so special? We are all righteously indignant when someone else holds in little esteem what we know to be precious. Extreme delight in someone or something naturally leads to extreme disgust when others consider that person or thing not worthy of their delight. No one who truly delights in God's word will be indifferent to the disregarding of it.

Second, he desires it. I count at least six times where the psalmist expresses his longing to keep the commands of God (vv. 5, 10, 17, 20, 40, 131). I count at least fourteen times when he expresses a desire to know and understand the word of God (vv. 18, 19, 27, 29, 33, 34, 35, 64, 66, 73, 124, 125, 135, 169). It's true for all of us: our lives are animated by desire. It's what literally gets us up in the morning. Desire is what we dream about, what we pray about, and what we think about when we are free to think about whatever we want to think about. Most of us have strong desires related to marriage, children, grandchildren, jobs, promotions, houses, vacations, revenge, recognition, and on and on. Some desires are good; some are bad. But consider, in that jumble of longings and passions, how strong is your desire to know and to understand and to keep the word of God? The psalmist so desired the word of God that he considered suffering to be a blessing in his life if it helped him become more obedient to God's commands (vv. 67–68, 71).

Third, he depends on it. The psalmist is constantly aware of his need for the word of God. "I cling to your testimonies,

O Lᴏʀᴅ; let me not be put to shame!" (v. 31). He is desperate for the encouragement found in God's promise and rules
(v. 50, 52). There are a lot of things we want in life, but there
are few things we really need. The word of God is one of those
things. In Amos's day the most severe punishment to fall on
the people of God was a "famine . . . of hearing the words of
the Lᴏʀᴅ" (Amos 8:11). There is no calamity like the silence
of God. We cannot know the truth or know ourselves or know
God's ways or savingly know God himself unless God speaks
to us. Every true Christian should feel deep in his bones an
utter dependence on God's self-revelation in the Scriptures.
Man does not live by bread alone, but by every word that
comes from the mouth of the Lord (Deut. 8:3; Matt. 4:4).

What we believe and feel about the word of God are absolutely crucial, if for no other reason than that they should
mirror what we believe and feel about Jesus. As we'll see,
Jesus believed unequivocally all that was written in the
Scriptures. If we are to be his disciples, we should believe
the same. Just as importantly, the New Testament teaches
that Jesus is the word made flesh, which means (among
other things) that all the attributes of God's verbal revelation
(truth, righteousness, power, veracity, wisdom, omniscience)
will be found in the person of Christ. All that the psalmist
believed and felt about the words from God is all that we
should feel and believe about the Word of God incarnate. Our
desire, delight, and dependence on the words of Scripture do
not grow inversely to our desire, delight, and dependence on
Jesus Christ. The two must always rise together. The most
mature Christians thrill to hear every love poem that speaks
about the Word made flesh *and* every love poem that cel-
ebrates the words of God.

What Should I Do with the Word of God?

The goal of this book is to get us believing what we should about the Bible, feeling what we should about the Bible, *and* to get us doing what we ought to do with the Bible. Given all that we've seen about the psalmist's faith in the word and passion for the word, it's no surprise that Psalm 119 is filled with action verbs illustrating the Spirit-prompted uses for the word:

- we sing the word (v. 172)
- speak the word (vv. 13, 46, 79)
- study the word (vv. 15, 48, 97, 148)
- store up the word (vv. 11, 93, 141)
- obey the word (vv. 8, 44, 57, 129, 145, 146, 167, 168)
- praise God for the word (vv. 7, 62, 164, 171)
- and pray that God would act according to his word (vv. 58, 121–123, 147, 149–152, 153–160)

These actions are no substitute for proper faith and affection, but they are the best indicators of what we really believe and feel about the word. Sing, speak, study, store up, obey, praise, and pray—this is how men and women of God handle the Scriptures. Now don't panic if you seem to fall short in believing, feeling, and doing. Remember, Psalm 119 is a love poem, not a checklist. The reason for starting with Psalm 119 is that this is where we want to end. This is the spiritual reaction the Spirit should produce in us when we fully grasp all that the Bible teaches about itself. My hope and prayer is that in some small way the rest of this book will help you say "Yes!" to what the psalmist believes, "Yes!" to what he feels, and "Yes!" to everything he does with God's holy and precious word.

A Few Final Clarifications

Before diving into the rest of the book, it might be helpful to know what type of book you are reading. While I hope this volume will motivate you to read the Bible, this is not a book on personal Bible study or principles for interpretation. Nor do I attempt an apologetic defense of Scripture, though I hope you will trust the Bible more for having read these eight chapters. This is not an exhaustive book, covering all the philosophical, theological, and methodological territory you might see in a fat, multivolume textbook. This is not an academic book with lots of footnotes. This is not a "take down" book where I name names and cite "chapter and verse" for current errors. This is not a groundbreaking work in exegetical, biblical, historical, or systematic theology.

"So what is this book?" you ask yourself, wondering how you managed to pick up such a know-nothing volume.

This is a book unpacking what the Bible says about the Bible. My aim is to be simple, uncluttered, straightforward, and manifestly biblical. I make no pretenses about offering you anything other than a doctrine of Scripture derived from Scripture itself. I know this raises questions about canon (how do you know you have the right Scriptures in the first place?) and questions about circular reasoning (how can you reference the Bible to determine the authority of the Bible?). These are reasonable questions, but they need not hold us up here. Both questions have to do with first principles, and a certain form of circularity is unavoidable whenever we try to defend our first principles. You can't establish the supreme authority of your supreme authority by going to some other lesser authority. Yes, the logic is circular, but no more so than the secularist defending reason by reason or the scientist touting the authority of science based on science. This doesn't mean Christians can be irrational and unreasonable in their views, but it does mean our first principle is neither rationality nor reason. We go the Bible to learn about the Bible because to judge the Bible by any other standard would be to make the Bible less than what it claims to be. As J. I. Packer wrote more than fifty years ago when facing similar challenges, "Scripture itself is alone competent to judge our doctrine of Scripture."[2]

There are many good books, some accessible and some technical, that thoughtfully explain and defend the canon of Scripture and the reliability of Scripture. I've listed several of them in the appendix. If you have doubts about how the books of the Bible proved to be self-authenticating, or doubts about the historical accuracy of the Bible, or doubts about the ancient biblical manuscripts, by all means study the issues for yourself. The claims of orthodox Christianity have no reason to avoid hard evidence and nothing to fear from a detailed examination of the facts.

But my conviction, born out of experience and derived from the teaching of Scripture itself, is that the most effective means for bolstering our confidence in the Bible is to spend time in the Bible. The Holy Spirit is committed to working through the word. God promises to bless the reading and teaching of his word. The sheep will hear their Master's voice speaking to them in the word (cf. John 10:27). In other words, the word of God is more than enough to accomplish the work of God in the people of God. There is no better way

---

[2] J. I. Packer, *"Fundamentalism" and the Word of God* (Grand Rapids, MI: Eerdmans, 1958), 76.

to understand and come to embrace a biblical doctrine of Scripture than to open the cage and let Scripture out.

If you've read this far, you probably have some interest in knowing the Bible better. You probably have some background in the Bible or have been directed here by someone who does. You may come with skepticism or full of faith, with ignorance needing to be remedied or with knowledge eager to be sharpened. Whatever the case, I trust, now that you know what kind of book this is, you'll be better prepared to benefit from it. And if you benefit from anything in these pages, it will be not because I've done anything wonderful, but because it is life-changing to come face-to-face with the world's most wonderful book.

May God give us ears, for we all need to hear the word of God more than God needs any of us to defend it.

2

Something More Sure

For we did not follow cleverly devised myths when we made known to you the power and coming of our Lord Jesus Christ, but we were eyewitnesses of his majesty. For when he received honor and glory from God the Father, and the voice was borne to him by the Majestic Glory, "This is my beloved Son, with whom I am well pleased," we ourselves heard this very voice borne from heaven, for we were with him on the holy mountain. And we have the prophetic word more fully confirmed, to which you will do well to pay attention as to a lamp shining in a dark place, until the day dawns and the morning star rises in your hearts, knowing this first of all, that no prophecy of Scripture comes from someone's own interpretation. For no prophecy was ever produced by the will of man, but men spoke from God as they were carried along by the Holy Spirit.

2 PETER 1:16–21

Several years ago there was an anonymous article in *Christianity Today* entitled "My Conversation with God." Here's how it began:

Does God still speak? I grew up hearing testimonies about it, but until October 2005, I couldn't say it had ever happened to me. I'm a middle-aged professor of theology at a well-known Christian university. I've written award-winning books. My name is on *Christianity Today's* masthead. For years I've taught that God still

speaks, but I couldn't testify to it personally. I can only
do so now anonymously, for reasons I hope will be clear.
A year after hearing God's voice, I still can't talk or even
think about my conversation with God without being
overcome by emotion.[1]

The anonymous professor went on to talk about an experience where God supernaturally gave him a book outline and
a book title and then directed him to use the money from the
book to help a young man go to school and prepare for ministry. He finished the article by saying how strengthened his
faith has been to finally have God personally speak to him.

It's a fine story in many ways, except in this crucial way: it
gives the impression that God does not normally speak to us
personally. The article leaves us feeling as though God speaking to us through the Scriptures is an inferior, less exciting,
less edifying means of communication. We can't help but conclude, "Yes, the Bible is important, but oh, what a treasure it
would be if I could experience God *really* speaking to me! If
only I could hear from the sure and infallible voice of God."

Sounds amazing, doesn't it? Can you imagine God speaking to you—personally, certainly, authoritatively? Well, the
good news (which the article seems to have missed) is that
every single one of us can hear from God *today*, right now, at
this very moment. God still speaks. And he has a word for us
that is sure, steady, and unerring.

Two Pieces of Evidence

Everything in that last sentence can be proven from the passage at the beginning of this chapter, 2 Peter 1:16–21. But

---

[1] http://www.christianitytoday.com/ct/2007/march/2.44.html.

in order to get to that conclusion, we have to understand the context for Peter's epistle.

The letter of 2 Peter is an exhortation to godliness. In verses 3–11 of chapter 1 we see the power for godliness in God's great and precious promises (vv. 3–4), the pattern for godliness in the virtues that can be added to faith (vv. 5–7), and the premise for godliness in our calling and election (vv. 8–11). Then in verses 12–15 Peter reiterates his intention to remind his readers of "these qualities" (i.e., the virtues of godliness) before he dies. Peter's concern is that false teachers will creep into the church, promising freedom, and will end up leading the people into sensuality and spiritual bondage instead (2:2, 10, 18–19). The exhortation, therefore, is to ignore these false teachers and pursue holiness.

And one of the chief reasons for doing so is the future coming of Christ. When the day of the Lord arrives, the world will be destroyed, our works exposed, and the ungodly judged (3:11–12, 14). In this epistle, and throughout the New Testament, the second coming of Christ serves as a profound motivation for turning aside from wickedness and making every effort to live an upright and virtuous life. We do not want to be found engaged in unholy deeds when the Holy One returns.

That's Peter's argument. But the false teachers doubted that the Lord would come again in some cataclysmic day of the Lord (3:2–4). They did not believe in a day of judgment. So Peter aims in his epistle to convince the faithful—contrary to the false teachers—that Christ is coming again to judge the living and the dead, and that this return will be a sight to behold.

To substantiate this claim, Peter offers two pieces of

evidence: eyewitness testimony (1:16–18) and authoritative documents (vv. 19–21). These were the two basic types of evidence in the ancient world, and not much has changed. Even today, you find lawyers usually making their case by submitting documents or calling on witnesses. If you want to prove your point in the court of law, you need eyewitness testimony or trustworthy sources. The apostle Peter had both.

We Ourselves Were with Him

Peter is sure of Christ's glorious return because he saw Christ transfigured in glory on the holy mountain. Peter, along with John and James, heard the Father's words and were eyewitnesses of the Son's majesty. Any one person who saw what they saw might have passed it off as hallucination or wishful thinking. But three men were on the mountain. They were there at the transfiguration, and they know beyond a doubt that Christ is not to be trifled with.

The language of 2 Peter 1:16 is important to Peter's argument and to our doctrine of Scripture. In recounting the events of the transfiguration, Peter makes clear that he does not follow "cleverly devised myths." Some liberal scholars have tried to use the category of "myth" to describe the Bible. They are quick to assert that "myth" is not the same as "false," and so they argue that while the *facts* of Scripture may not always be believable, the larger, deeper *truth* still is. So, for example, they'd suggest that the plagues in Exodus and the crossing of the Red Sea may not be historical, but that need not call into question the power of God or his ability to set the captives free. Jesus may or may not have walked on water, but no matter: the important point is that he will do anything to help us if we trust in him. The resurrection of Christ, some liberals argue, is not to be taken literally as a bodily resurrection, but rather as a powerful symbol that God can give us new spiritual life and snatch victory from the jaws of defeat.

This kind of thinking is still very pervasive. Once I got into a blog exchange with a liberal pastor who questioned the historicity of the virgin birth. We went back and forth several times until we realized we were operating from different conceptual worlds. "Do I think the virgin birth is essential to our creed as Christians?" he wrote. "That's not really mine to say, is it? As you say, it has been confessed for centuries, and thus, I need to take it seriously and to heart and to wrestle with how I understand it." The ambiguous (and functionally useless) language of taking the virgin birth "seriously" and needing "to wrestle" with his understanding of it was already frustrating. And then I got to his conclusion: "For my part, I take the statement 'all things are possible with God' as more valuable to my faith than 'how can this be, since I am still a virgin?' I don't claim that you need to accept my understanding, nor would I imagine that you would claim that I must necessarily accept your understanding." My reply was something to the effect that "I *do* claim that you need to accept my understanding, because it's not my understanding. It's the teaching of the New Testament and the affirmation of the orthodox Christian church throughout the centuries."

Besides displaying a self-defeating logic—if all things really are possible with God, why choke on a miraculous virgin birth?—the liberal understanding of history is completely at odds with the Bible's own self-understanding. The Greek word *mythos* is always used negatively in the New Testament (see 1 Tim. 1:4; 4:7; 2 Tim. 4:4; Titus 1:14). Myth is seen as the opposite of truth. "For the time is coming," Paul warns, "when people will not endure sound teaching, but having itching ears they will accumulate for themselves teachers to suit their own passions, and will turn away from listening to the truth and wander off into myths" (2 Tim. 4:3–4). For the biblical writers, there is myth on one side and truth on the other, and the Bible clearly belongs with the latter.

Even if it is argued that the liberal definition of myth is not exactly what the New Testament is condemning when it critiques "myths," you still can't get around the logic of 2 Peter 1:16. In referencing his role as an eyewitness, Peter wants everyone to know that the Jesus story—the transfiguration primarily, but presumably also the rest of the gospel story he passed down—is in the category of historical, verifiable fact, not impressions, or inner experiences, or stories invented to make a point. The Greeks and Romans had lots of myths. They didn't care whether the stories were literally true. No one was interested in the historical evidence for the claim that Hercules was the illegitimate son of Zeus. It was a myth, a fable, a tall tale, a story to entertain and make sense of the world. Paganism was built on the power of mythology, but Christianity, like the Jewish faith from which it sprang, saw itself as an entirely different kind of religion.

This cannot be stated too strongly: From the very beginning, Christianity tied itself to history. The most important claims of Christianity are historical claims, and on the facts of history the Christian religion must stand or fall. Luke followed all things closely, researched things carefully, and relied on eyewitnesses so that Theophilus could have "certainty" about the gospel story (Luke 1:1–4). John wrote about the wonders Jesus performed so that his audience would accept the miracles, understand the signs, believe that Jesus is the Christ, and have life in his name (John 20:31). All four Gospel writers are eager for us to know that, though some were spreading rumors that Christ's body had been stolen after his crucifixion, the tomb was really empty because Jesus had really been raised. If Christ wasn't raised, said Paul, the whole Christian religion is a sham and those who believe in it are pitiable fools (1 Cor. 15:14–19). To discount history is to live in a different world from the one that the biblical authors inhabit.

It's as if Peter is saying, "Look, I saw the transfiguration, and I was not alone. We heard it. We were eyewitnesses and ear-witnesses. We are not making this up to scare you. We are not passing along intriguing stories or clever tales. We are telling you what happened. We saw his glory. We saw it with our own eyes. We heard God speak—audibly. This was not an experience in our hearts or a vision in our souls. If you had been on the mountain, you would have seen and heard the same things. We are talking about fact, not fable."

Remember the point Peter is trying to make. This is not some dry, abstract apologetics textbook. He wants the saints to be holy. He wants them to consider their lives in light of Christ's return. He is trying to convince them of the certainty of the second coming. And one way to prove that a glorious, dreadful, amazing, wonderful, fearful second coming of Christ will happen in history is for Peter to remind these believers that he has already seen a glorious, dreadful, amazing, wonderful, fearful appearing of Christ. Peter saw the unveiling. He saw what Jesus looked like in his full divine regalia. Peter realized Christ was more than a carpenter, more than an open-minded guru, more than a nonjudgmental encourager of everyone and everything. When he saw Jesus sparkle white and dazzle in majesty with the glory cloud, he knew at that moment that this was not a man to be trifled with. And when Jesus comes again we will all realize, even if it is too late for some, that ungodly living is inconsistent with the glory of Christ. That's Peter's point, and it depends on history, on the evidence of eyewitness testimony.

It Is Written

Peter's point about the return of Christ also depends on the trustworthiness of authoritative documents (2 Pet. 1:19–21). The "prophetic word" is prior to Peter's own eyewitness account. And whatever Peter, James, and John saw on the mountain, and whatever it portended about the second coming of Christ and the last judgment, these things only confirmed what the prophetic word had already made sure (v. 19). You cannot put more confidence in your Bible than Peter put in his.

Notice three truths these verses teach us about the nature of Scripture.

First, Scripture is the word of God. This may sound like a redundant statement, but the *is* says something important. Some Christians, influenced by neoorthodox theologians like Karl Barth, are hesitant to say the Bible *is* the word of God. Instead, they argue that the Bible *contains* the word of God, or *becomes* the word of God, or that the *event* in which God speaks to us through the Bible is the word of God. Neoorthodox thinking attempts to distance claims of inspiration from the written words on the pages of Scripture. This distinction, however, would have been foreign to the apostle Peter, for all the lofty claims he makes about "prophecy" or the "prophetic word" are made with reference to the written words of Scripture.

Peter uses three different terms to refer to the word of God in these verses: the "prophetic word" (v. 19), "prophecy of Scripture" (v. 20), and "prophecy" (v. 21). They all mention prophecy in some way and are used more or less interchangeably. Importantly, for our considerations, the Greek word in verse 20 for Scripture is *graphe*, which refers to something that has been written down. Peter has in mind for verse 20 not just oral traditions or a speech event, but a written text. Peter's view of inspiration cannot be limited to prophetic speech or a preaching event; it includes the pages of Scripture.

And not just the prophetic parts about the second coming. The whole Old Testament is in view. Just as "the Law and the Prophets" can be a general designation for the Old Testament (cf. Matt. 7:12), so can the law *or* the prophets separately. No Jew would make a distinction that some parts of Scripture were truer parts than others (cf. 2 Tim. 3:16). Whatever is true of the law is true of the prophets, and vice versa. The "prophetic word" is simply a way of referring to inscripturated revelation. As Calvin says, "[I] understand by prophecy of Scripture that which is contained in the holy Scriptures."[2]

All of this matters because it means the authority of God's word resides in the written text—the words, the sentences, the paragraphs—of Scripture, not merely in our existential

---

[2] John Calvin, *Commentaries on the Catholic Epistles*, trans. and ed. John Owen (Grand Rapids, MI: Baker, 1993 [1855]), 391.

experience of the truth in our hearts. Some people don't like written texts and propositions because they imply a stable, fixed meaning, and people don't want truth to be fixed. They would rather have inspiration be more subjective, more internal, more experiential. But according to 2 Peter 1:19–21, the inspiration of holy Scripture is an objective reality outside of us.

None of this is to suggest that an evangelical theory of inspiration leads us away from the subjective, internal, or experiential. Quite the contrary. We are to "pay attention" to the inspired Scriptures as to "a lamp shining in a dark place" (v. 19). God's word convicts us of sin, shows us the way, and leads us from darkness into light. We immerse ourselves in Scripture so that the morning star, Christ himself (see Num. 24:17–19; cf. Rev. 22:16), would rise in our hearts. The goal of revelation is not information only, but affection, worship, and obedience. Christ *in* us will be realized only as we drink deeply of the Bible, which is God's word outside of us.

Second, the word of God is no less divine because it is given through human instrumentality. Many have claimed and continue to claim that conservative Christians hold to a mechanical dictation theory of inspiration. Evangelicals, it is said, believe the writers of the Bible were passive instruments who merely recorded what they were given by rote from heaven. Despite the frequency of this claim, I've never found any evangelical theologian who describes inspiration in this way. It's true that older theologians sometimes spoke of the Scriptures as being so flawless that it's *as if* they were given by dictation. The metaphor (which is probably more misleading than helpful) was meant to underscore the Bible's perfection, but it was not meant to describe the actual process whereby the authors of the Bible wrote their inspired texts. Rather, 2 Peter 1:21 teaches, as evangelical theologians have emphasized over and over, that men spoke (and wrote) as they were "carried along" by the Holy Spirit.

The phrase "concursive operation" is often used to describe the process of inspiration, meaning that God used the intellect, skills, and personality of fallible men to write down what was divine and infallible. The Bible is, in one sense, both a human and a divine book. But this in no way implies any fallibility in the Scriptures. The dual authorship of Scripture does not necessitate imperfection any more than the two natures of Christ mean our Savior must have sinned. As Calvin says about the prophets, "[they] dared not to announce anything of their own, and obediently followed the Spirit as their guide, who ruled in their mouth as in his own sanctuary."[3]

The verb "carried" in verse 21 is *phero*, which is translated as "produced" earlier in the same verse and as "borne" in verses 17 and 18. It suggests an assured outcome, one that is carried out and guaranteed by another. The words from heaven (vv. 17–18) and the words from the prophets (v. 21) ultimately came from the same place: God.

B. B. Warfield explains,

> The term here used [for carried/borne] is a very specific one. It is not to be confounded with guiding, or directing, or controlling, or even leading in the full sense of that word. It goes beyond all such terms, in assigning the effect produced specifically to the active agent. What is "borne" is taken up by the "bearer" and conveyed by the

---

[3] Ibid.

"bearer's" power, not its own, to the "bearer's" goal, not its own. The men who spoke from God are here declared, therefore, to have been taken up by the Holy Spirit and brought by His power to the goal of His choosing. The things which they spoke under this operation of the Spirit were therefore His things, not theirs. And that is the reason which is assigned why "the prophetic word" is so sure. Though spoken through the instrumentality of men, it is, by virtue of the fact that these men spoke "as borne by the Holy Spirit," an immediately Divine word.[4]

The divine authorship of the Scriptures does not preclude the use of active human instrumentation, just as human participation does not render the Scriptures any less perfect and divine.

Third, the Bible is without error. The Scriptures do not come from human interpretation (2 Pet. 1:20). The ideas did not spring forth from the confused mind of man. More than that, Peter testifies that no prophecy was ever produced by the "will of man" (v. 21). We must come to the Bible, Calvin teaches, with a reverence that exists only "when we are convinced that God speaks to us, and not mortal men."[5] We must believe the prophecies "as the indubitable oracles of God, because they have not emanated from men's own private suggestions."[6] The ultimate authorship of Scripture, Peter informs us, is God himself.

---

[4] Benjamin B. Warfield, *The Inspiration and Authority of the Bible* (Phillipsburg, NJ: Presbyterian & Reformed, 1948), 137. To be precise, Warfield sees three modes of revelation in Scripture: external manifestation, internal suggestion, and concursive operation (83–96). He places the Old Testament prophetic ministry in the second category, seeing the prophets as more passive than the apostolic authors of the New Testament. Nevertheless, he warns against pressing the distinctions too far, noting that the prophets still used their intelligence in receiving God's word, and the entire Scriptures are described as "prophecy" in 2 Peter 1:19–21. See also the "Bibliology" section in Fred G. Zaspel, *Theology of B. B. Warfield: A Systematic Summary* (Wheaton, IL: Crossway, 2010).
[5] Calvin, *Commentaries on the Catholic Epistles*, 390.
[6] Ibid.

There are many texts we could use to show that the Bible is without error, but here's the simplest argument: Scripture did not come from the will of man; it came from God. And if it is God's word then it must all be true, for in him there can be no error or deceit.

Inerrancy means the word of God always stands over us and we never stand over the word of God. When we reject inerrancy we put ourselves in judgment over God's word. We claim the right to determine which parts of God's revelation can be trusted and which cannot. When we deny the complete trustworthiness of the Scriptures—in its claims with regard to history; its teachings on the material world; its miracles; in the tiniest "jots and tittles" of all that it affirms—then we are forced to accept one of two conclusions: either Scripture is not all from God, or God is not always dependable. To make either statement is to affirm a sub-Christian point of view. These conclusions do not express a proper submission to the Father, do not work for our joy in Christ, and do not bring honor to the Spirit, who carried along the men to speak the prophetic word and to author God's holy book.

Defending the doctrine of inerrancy may seem like a fool's errand to some and a divisive shibboleth to others, but, in truth, the doctrine is at the heart of our faith. To deny, disregard, edit, alter, reject, or rule out anything in God's word is to commit the sin of unbelief. "Let God be true though every one were a liar" must be our rallying cry (Rom. 3:4). Finding a halfway house where some things in the Bible are true and other things (as we have judged them) are not is an impossibility. This kind of compromised Christianity, besides flying in the face of the Bible's own self-understanding, does not satisfy the soul or present to the lost the sort of God they need to meet. How are we to believe in a God who can do the unimaginable and forgive our trespasses, conquer our sins, and give us hope in a dark world if we cannot believe that this God created the world out of nothing, gave the virgin a child, and raised his Son on the third day? "One cannot doubt the Bible," J. I. Packer warns, "without far-reaching loss, both of fullness of truth and of fullness of life. If therefore we have at heart spiritual renewal for society, for churches and for our own lives, we shall make much of the entire trust-worthiness—that is, the inerrancy—of Holy Scripture as the inspired and liberating Word of God."[7]

Nothing More Sure

The word of God is true. The good news of Jesus Christ has been recorded in the facts of history. There was a man born of a woman in Bethlehem. Thousands of people saw him and knew him. He did miracles witnessed by multitudes. He died, rose again, and appeared to more than five hundred witnesses (1 Cor. 15:6). Everyone knew the location of the tomb, and it was empty and open to examination. Three disciples in particular were eyewitnesses of his majesty on the Mount of Transfiguration. They saw that event, and simply passed on what they or their closest associates had also seen.

We do not follow myths. We are not interested in stories with a nice moral to them. We are not helped by hoping in spiritual possibilities which we know to be historically impossible. These things in the gospel story happened. God predicted them. He fulfilled them. He inspired the written

---

[7] J. I. Packer, *Truth and Power: The Place of Scripture in the Christian Life* (Wheaton, IL: Harold Shaw, 1996), 55.

record of them. Therefore we ought to believe them. Nothing in all of the Bible was produced solely by the human will. God used men to write the words, but these men did their work carried along by the Holy Spirit. The Bible is an utterly reliable book, an unerring book, a holy book, a divine book.

Do not miss the staggering claim in 2 Peter 1:19. After going into great detail about the awesome events on the Mount of Transfiguration, after taking great pains to explain that he was an eyewitness to these things, after laboring to show us that he is speaking rock-solid, historically verifiable truth, after all this Peter says we now have the "prophetic word more fully confirmed." The inscripturated word of God was already true as true can be; Peter's testimony only *confirmed* what was already sure.

Some scholars think verse 19 should be translated "and we have something more sure." In fact, this is how an earlier edition of the ESV translated the verse. In that case, Peter could be seen as saying that the prophetic word of Scripture was a surer testimony than his eyewitness account of the transfiguration. He would be saying, "If you don't trust my eyes, trust the prophetic word. The Scriptures are more reliable than my senses." But even if we stick with the updated ESV translation for verse 19, the point of verses 19–21 is not changed. Whether the prophetic word is, for Peter, confirmed by what he saw or is more sure than what he saw, his view of Scripture is the same. There is no more authoritative declaration than what we find in the word of God, no firmer ground to stand on, no "more final" argument that can be spoken after Scripture has spoken.

Do you talk about Scripture the way the apostles talked about Scripture? You can think too highly of your interpretations of Scripture, but you cannot think too highly of Scripture's interpretation of itself. You can exaggerate your authority in handling the Scriptures, but you cannot exaggerate the Scriptures' authority to handle you. You can use the word of God to come to wrong conclusions, but you cannot find any wrong conclusions in the word of God.

You do not need another special revelation from God outside the Bible. You can listen to the voice of God every day. Christ still speaks, because the Spirit has already spoken. If you want to hear from God, go to the book that records only what he has said. Immerse yourself in the word of God. You will not find anything more sure.

God's Word Is Enough

Long ago, at many times and in many ways, God spoke to our fathers by the prophets, but in these last days he has spoken to us by his Son, whom he appointed the heir of all things, through whom also he created the world. He is the radiance of the glory of God and the exact imprint of his nature, and he upholds the universe by the word of his power. After making purification for sins, he sat down at the right hand of the Majesty on high, having become as much superior to angels as the name he has inherited is more excellent than theirs.

HEBREWS 1:1–4

Have you ever wondered if the Bible is really able to help you with your deepest problems? Have you struggled to know what to do with your life, and wished you had some special word from the Lord? Have you ever thought to yourself that the biblical teaching on sexuality needs updating? Have you ever wished for a more direct, more personal revelation than what you get from slowly reading through the Bible? Have you ever secretly wanted to add something to the word of God—you know, just to make things safer? Have you ever wanted to take something away to make the Bible more palatable? Have you ever assumed that the Bible doesn't say anything about how to worship God or how to order his church? Have you ever felt like the Bible just wasn't enough for living a faithful life in today's world? If you can answer yes to any of these questions—and we all will at times—then you are struggling with the *sufficiency* of Scripture.

Most Christians are familiar with the attributes of God. At some point and at some level we've studied God's holiness, justice, omniscience, sovereignty, goodness, mercy, love, and whatever other characteristics might be listed as divine attributes. But I doubt that we could name, much less explain, the attributes of *Scripture*. Traditionally, Protestant theologians have highlighted four essential characteristics of Scripture: sufficiency, clarity, authority, and necessity. Each of the attributes—you can recall them by the handy acronym SCAN—is meant to protect an important truth about the Bible:

Sufficiency: The Scriptures contain everything we need for knowledge of salvation and godly living. We don't need any new revelation from heaven.

Clarity: The saving message of Jesus Christ is plainly taught in the Scriptures and can be understood by all who have ears to hear it. We don't need an official magisterium to tell us what the Bible means.

Authority: The last word always goes to the word of God. We must never allow the teachings of science, of human experience, or of church councils to take precedence over Scripture.

Necessity: General revelation is not enough to save us. We cannot know God savingly by means of personal experience and human reason. We need God's word to tell us how to live, who Christ is, and how to be saved.

Or to rearrange the order of the attributes, we could say: God's word is final; God's word is understandable; God's word is necessary; and God's word is enough. Each of these attributes deserves a chapter of its own. We'll start in this chapter with the sufficiency of Scripture.

More than Enough

The doctrine of the sufficiency of Scripture—sometimes called the perfection of Scripture—means that "Scripture is clear enough to make us responsible for carrying out our present responsibilities to God."[1] It's an ethical doctrine. It takes away any excuses for disobedience. No one can say God has not revealed enough for us to be saved or to live a life pleasing to him. Scripture makes us competent and "equipped for *every* good work" (2 Tim. 3:16–17). We do not need to add to it to meet today's challenges or subtract from it to mesh with today's ideals. The word of God is perfect and complete, giving us all we need to know about Christ, salvation, and godliness. Or as the church father Athanasius put it, "The sacred and divinely inspired Scriptures are sufficient for the exposition of the truth."[2]

Of the four attributes of Scripture, this may be the one that evangelicals forget first. If authority is the liberal problem, clarity the postmodern problem, and necessity the problem for atheists and agnostics, then sufficiency is the attribute most quickly doubted by rank-and-file churchgoing Christians. We can say all the right things about the Bible,

---

[1] John M. Frame, *The Doctrine of the Word of God* (Philipsburg, NJ: Presbyterian & Reformed, 2010), 226.
[2] Quoted in Timothy Ward, *Words of Life: Scripture as the Living and Active Word of God* (Downers Grove, IL: IVP Academic, 2009), 107.

and even read it regularly, but when life gets difficult, or just a bit boring, we look for new words, new revelation, and new experiences to bring us closer to God. We feel rather ho-hum about the New Testament's description of heaven, but we are mesmerized by the accounts of school-age children who claim to have gone there and back. From magazine articles about "My Conversation with God" (see chapter 2), to best-selling books where God is depicted as giving special, private communications, we can easily operate as if the Bible were not enough. If we could only have something *more* than the Scriptures, then we would be really close to Jesus and know his love for us.

Unless, of course, the finality of Christ's redemption for us is intimately tied to the finality of his revelation to us.

God's Superior Son

The big idea in the first verses of Hebrews is the big idea for the whole book of Hebrews. God has spoken by his Son, and this Son is superior to all persons, heavenly beings, institutions, rituals, and previous means of revelation and redemption. That's why verses 1 and 2 begin with a series of contrasts.

Eras. The age gone by was "long ago," but now we are in "these last days." This does not necessarily mean the end of the world is coming soon. It means we have entered a new age, the age of the Spirit, the fullness of time in which the great acts of salvation have taken place. The death and resurrection of Jesus ushered the world into a different epoch. There is no act of redemption left to take place before the last day arrives. That puts us *in* the last days.

Recipients. In an earlier time, long ago, God spoke "to our fathers"—to the patriarchs, to the Jewish ancestors. But in these days God has spoken "to us." This is a different age, and God is speaking to a different group of people.

Agents. God has also spoken by a different "agency." In previous days he spoke by "the prophets," whether the named prophets of old, those with a prophetic function like Moses, or the prophetic writings (i.e., the Old Testament Scriptures). "By the prophets" is how God has spoken. But in these last days God has spoken "by his Son." Jesus Christ has revealed what God is like, taught us the will of God, and shown us the path of salvation.

Ways. Long ago God spoke at many times (*polymeros*) and in many ways (*polytropos*). God spoke by visions, dreams, voices, a burning bush, a pillar of fire, a donkey, and writing on a wall. That was then, in the old age. But in these last days God has spoken in a single way, by the Lord Jesus Christ. The implicit contrast is that whereas there were many ways formerly in which God spoke to his people, there is now only one means of revelation: through his Son.

All four contrasts are meant to lead us to the same conclusion, a conclusion gloriously spelled out in verses 2–4 of Hebrews 1—namely, that Christ is the superior and final agent of God's redemption and revelation. The writer of Hebrews, drawing from Psalms 2 and 110, makes seven affirmations to this end:

1. *The Son is the heir of all things* (Heb. 1:2b). Everything culminates in Christ. The mission work of this age is to bring to Christ what rightfully belongs to him.

2. *The Son is the creator of all things* (v. 2c). Though the second person of the Trinity is not mentioned by name in the creation account, we see in Genesis that God created by the action of his divine speech. This word spoken is to be identified with the Word who later became incarnate.

3. *The Son is the sustainer of all things* (v. 3a). Every proton, every electron, every compound, every particle and planet, every star and galaxy is upheld by his powerful word.

4. *The Son is the revelation of God* (v. 3a). He is the manifestation of God's presence, not merely a reflection of the divine glory but the radiance of it. He is the exact imprint of God, same in essence and nature. Christ shows us God as he truly is.

5. *The Son made purification for our sins* (v. 3b). He took away the stain and guilt of sin, not just as a shadow of greater things to come (like the former sacrifices) but as the substance of all that had been prefigured.

6. *The Son sat down* (v. 3b). Just as a mother sits down at the end of the day because the kids are finally in bed and the kitchen is clean, so Christ sat down at the right hand of God because his work had been accomplished. The enthronement was complete (Ps. 110:1) and the priestly task completed once for all (Heb. 9:25–26).

7. *The Son, therefore, has become much superior to angels* (v. 4). He is superior to these heavenly messengers because God's final word has been spoken through him. None will come after him. Our great salvation has come—confirmed by signs, wonders, miracles, and gifts of the Spirit—and it shall never be surpassed (2:1–4).

God has spoken by his Son, and this Son is superior to all persons, heavenly beings, institutions, rituals, and previous means of revelation and redemption. That's the big idea in Hebrews 1:1–4 and throughout the book. Christ is superior to angels (chs. 1–2), to Moses (ch. 3), to Joshua (chs. 3–4), to Aaron (ch. 5), to Abraham (ch. 6), to Melchizedek (ch. 7), to the old covenant (ch. 8), to the tabernacle (ch. 9), to the high priest (ch. 10), to the treasures of this world (ch. 11), to Mount Sinai (ch. 12), and to the city we have here on earth (ch. 13). The Son is our Great Superlative, surpassing all others because in him we have the fullness and finality of God's redemption and revelation.

Sufficiency in the Son and in the Scriptures

So what does any of this have to do with the sufficiency of Scripture? Look more closely at the conclusion just stated above: the Son is superior to all others because in him we have the fullness and finality of God's redemption and revelation. We do pretty well understanding the *fullness* piece. Everything in the days "long ago" was pointing to Christ, and everything was completed in Christ. He is the fulfillment of centuries of predications, prophecies, and types. That's the fullness part of the equation.

But just as important is the *finality* of Christ's work. God has definitively made himself known. Christ has once for all paid for our sins. He came to earth, lived among us, died on the cross, and cried out in his dying moments, "It is finished!" We are awaiting no other king to rule over us. We need no other prophet like Muhammad. There can be no further priest to atone for our sins. The work of redemption has been completed.

And we must not separate redemption from revelation. Both were finished and fulfilled in the Son. The word of God versus the Word of God? The Bible versus Jesus? The Scriptures versus the Son? Hebrews gives no room for these diabolical antitheses. True, the Bible is not Jesus; the Scripture is not the Son. The words of the Bible and the Word made flesh are distinct, but they are also inseparable. Every act of redemption—from the exodus, to the return from exile, to the cross itself—is also a revelation. They tell us something about the nature of sin, the way of salvation, and the character of God. Likewise, the point of revelation is always to redeem. The words of the prophets and the apostles are not meant to make us smart, but to get us saved. Redemption reveals. Revelation redeems.

And Christ is both. He is God's full and final act of redemption and God's full and final revelation of himself. Even the later teachings of the apostles were simply the remembrances of what Christ said (John 14:26) and the further Spirit-wrought explanation of all that he was and all that he accomplished (John 16:13–15). "Nothing can be added to his redemptive work," Frame argues, "and nothing can be added to the revelation of that redemptive work."[3] If we say revelation is not complete, we must admit that somehow the work of redemption also remains unfinished.

So are we saying that God no longer speaks? Not at all. But we must think carefully about how he speaks in these last days. God now speaks through his Son. Think about

---

[3] Frame, *Doctrine of the Word of God*, 227.

the three offices of Christ—prophet, priest, and king. In a very real sense, Christ has finished his work in each of these three offices. And yet he continues to work *through* that finished work.

As a king, Christ is already seated on the throne and already reigns from heaven, but the inauguration of his kingdom is not the same as the consummation of it. There are still enemies to subdue under his feet (Heb. 2:8).

As a priest, Christ has fully paid for all our sins with his precious blood, once for all, never to be repeated again. And yet, this great salvation must still be freely offered, and Christ must keep us in it (Heb. 2:3).

Finally, as a prophet, God has decisively spoken in his Son. He has shown us all we need to know, believe, and do. There is nothing more to say. And yet, God keeps speaking through what he has already said. "The word of God is living and active" (Heb. 4:12); and when the Scriptures are read, the Holy Spirit still speaks (3:7).

So, yes, God still speaks. He is not silent. He communicates with us personally and directly. But this ongoing speech is not ongoing revelation. "The Holy Spirit no longer reveals any new doctrines but takes everything from Christ (John 16:14)," Bavinck writes. "In Christ God's revelation has been completed."[4] In these last days, God speaks to us not by many and various ways, but in one way, through his Son. And he speaks through his Son by the revelation of the Son's redeeming work that we find first predicted and prefigured in the Old Testament, then recorded in the Gospels,

---

[4] Herman Bavinck, *Reformed Dogmatics, Volume 1: Prolegomena*, ed. John Bolt, trans. John Vriend (Grand Rapids, MI: Baker Academic, 2003), 491.

and finally unpacked by the Spirit through the apostles in the rest of the New Testament.

Scripture is enough because the work of Christ is enough. They stand or fall together. The Son's redemption and the Son's revelation must both be sufficient. And as such, there is nothing more to be done and nothing more to be known for our salvation and for our Christian walk than what we see and know about Christ and through Christ in his Spirit's book. Frame is right: "Scripture is God's testimony to the redemption he has accomplished for us. Once that redemption is finished, and the apostolic testimony to it is finished, the Scriptures are complete, and we should expect no more additions to them."[5] Or as Packer put it, more tersely but no less truly, "There are no words of God spoken to us at all today except the words of Scripture."[6]

Practical Sufficiency

And why does any of this matter? What difference does the sufficiency of Scripture make for your Christian life? Let me finish the chapter by suggesting four ways it ought to make a huge difference.

First, with the sufficiency of Scripture we keep tradition in its place. Tradition certainly has a place in understanding God's word and formulating the church's doctrinal convictions. The diversity most easily overlooked today is the diversity of the dead. We should learn from the great teachers who

---

[5] Frame, *Doctrine of the Word of God*, 227.

[6] J. I. Packer, *"Fundamentalism" and the Word of God* (Grand Rapids, MI: Eerdmans, 1958), 119. While this kind of "immediate" revelation has ceased, we should allow for "mediate" revelation whereby God gives us new insights and applications—sometimes in surprising ways—but always through Scripture. See Garnet Milne, *The Westminster Confession of Faith and the Cessation of Special Revelation: The Majority Puritan Viewpoint on Whether Extra-Biblical Prophecy Is Still Possible* (Bletchley, Milton Keynes, UK: Paternoster, 2007).

have come before us. We should stand fast on the ecumenical creeds of the church. And for those of us in confessional traditions—like Lutherans, Anglicans, Presbyterians, and the Reformed—we must take the vows to uphold our confessional standards seriously, carefully, and with integrity. But even these great creeds, catechisms, and confessions are valuable only as they summarize what is taught in Scripture. No secondary, man-made text can replace or be allowed to subvert our allegiance to and knowledge of the Bible.

The sufficiency of Scripture undergirds the Reformation cry of *sola Scriptura*, or "Scripture alone." This doesn't mean we try to approach the Bible without the help of good teachers, scholarly resources, and tested doctrinal formulas. "Alone" does not mean "by itself" (*solo Scriptura*) apart from any communal or confessional considerations, but that Scripture alone is the final authority. Everything must be tested against the word of God. Tradition does not have an equal role with the Bible in our knowing the truth. Rather, tradition has a confirmatory, illuminating, and supportive role to play. We cannot accept doctrinal innovations like papal infallibility, purgatory, the immaculate conception, or the veneration of Mary, because these doctrines cannot be found in the word of God and they contradict what *is* revealed in Scripture. Although we may respect our Catholic friends and be thankful for many aspects of their faith and social witness, we must not waver in our allegiance to *sola Scriptura*. It is implicit in the biblical understanding of its own sufficiency.

Second, because Scripture is sufficient, we will not add to or subtract from the word of God. When coming to the Bible, we must always remember we are reading a covenantal book. And covenantal documents typically conclude

3

with a covenantal inscription curse. We see such a curse in Deuteronomy 4:2 and 12:32, where the Israelites are warned against adding to the Mosaic law or taking anything away from it (cf. Prov. 30:5–6). Likewise, we see the same kind of curse at the conclusion of the New Testament in Revelation 22:18–19—"I warn everyone who hears the words of the prophecy of this book: if anyone adds to them, God will add to him the plagues described in this book, and if anyone takes away from the words of the book of this prophecy, God will take away his share in the tree of life and in the holy city, which are described in this book." This strong admonition, at the end of the whole Bible no less, is a strong reminder that we must not add anything to the Scriptures—to make them better, safer, or more in line with our assumptions—and we must not subtract anything from them, even if experience, academic journals, or the mood of the culture insist that we must.

Third, since the Bible is sufficient, we can expect the word of God to be relevant to all of life. God has given us all we need for life and godliness (2 Peter 1:3); Scripture is enough to make us wise for salvation and holy unto the Lord (2 Tim. 3:14–17). If we learn to read the Bible down (into our hearts), across (the plot line of Scripture), out (to the end of the story), and up (to the glory of God in the face of Christ), we will find that every bit of the Bible is profitable for us. To affirm the sufficiency of Scripture is not to suggest that the Bible tells us everything we want to know about everything, but it does tell us everything we need to know about what matters most. Scripture does not give exhaustive information on every subject, but in every subject on which it speaks, it says only what is true. And in its truth we have enough knowledge to turn from sin, find a Savior, make good decisions, please God, and get to the root of our deepest problems.

Fourth, the doctrine of the sufficiency of Scripture invites us to open our Bibles to hear the voice of God. Not long ago I was in a denominational advisory group where we were told to find our "norms" as a community. When I suggested our first norm should be testing everything against the word of God, I was told—and this is an exact quote—that "we are not here to open our Bibles." The goal of the group, apparently, was that we would listen to our hearts and listen to each other, but not so much that we would listen to God. Later at the same denominational meeting, a pastor from South America addressed the whole body. Upon noticing an advertisement in the back for an event where we would "discover" God's vision for our denomination, the man remarked, "Discover? I hope you find what you are looking for. And try not to take too long." It was a well-placed dig at the tendency in the American church to plan and dream and scheme and vision-cast and engage in mutual discernment, all while God's clear voice lies neglected on our laps.

The word of God is more than enough for the people of God to live their lives to the glory of God. The Father will speak by means of all that the Spirit has spoken through the Son. The question is whether we will open our Bibles and bother to listen.

4

God's Word Is Clear

For this commandment that I command you today is not too hard for you, neither is it far off. It is not in heaven, that you should say, "Who will ascend to heaven for us and bring it to us, that we may hear it and do it?" Neither is it beyond the sea, that you should say, "Who will go over the sea for us and bring it to us, that we may hear it and do it?" But the word is very near you. It is in your mouth and in your heart, so that you can do it.

DEUTERONOMY 30:11–14

Several years ago I was speaking on a panel about the emergent church. Along with the other panelists, I was in a massive conference room that could have seated at least a thousand people. It was a back-and-forth, debate-like atmosphere, with a robust seventy-five people barely paying attention as they were spread out in the cavernous hall. Although the event was eminently forgettable, I remember that session because of the man who came up to talk to me afterward. Actually, "talk" would be a euphemism. It was more like a harangue. This man, whose wife was standing off to the side with an "I've seen this before" expression on her face, was furious because I dared to claim that I knew what Scripture taught.

I quickly realized our conversation was going nowhere

and was only frustrating both of us. Anytime I would bring up a text of Scripture, he would say, "Well, that's just your interpretation." Then I would bring up other Scriptures to show that Jesus and the apostles claimed to know what Scripture meant, and he would say, "Well, that's just your interpretation of those passages about interpreting Scripture." Then I would talk about Paul reasoning in the synagogue, and he would say, "That's only your way of understanding that story." You can see why the conversation wasn't very meaningful. We couldn't talk about any other important issues because we did not agree on whether we could know anything for certain from the Bible. In short, we did not share the same understanding of the clarity of Scripture.

A Careful Definition

The clarity of Scripture—sometimes known by the older word "perspicuity" (which, for a word that means clarity, is not all that clear)—is carefully defined in the Westminster Confession of Faith (WCF):

> All things in Scripture are not alike plain in themselves, nor alike clear unto all: yet those things which are necessary to be known, believed, and observed for salvation, are so clearly propounded, and opened in some place of Scripture or other, that not only the learned, but the unlearned, in a due use of the ordinary means, may attain unto a sufficient understanding of them. (WCF 1.7)

It's worth noticing several important nuances in this definition.

- Some portions of Scripture are clearer than others. Not every passage has a simple or obvious meaning.
- The main things we need to know, believe, and do can be clearly seen in the Bible.
- Though the most essential doctrines are not equally clear in every passage, they are all made clear somewhere in Scripture.
- That which is necessary for our salvation can be understood even by the uneducated, provided that they make use of the ordinary means of study and learning.
- The most important points in the Scriptures may not be understood perfectly, but they can be understood sufficiently.

The doctrine of the clarity of Scripture is not a wild assertion that the meaning of every verse in the Bible will be patently obvious to everyone. Rather, the perspicuity of Scripture upholds the notion that ordinary people using ordinary means can accurately understand enough of what must be known, believed, and observed for them to be faithful Christians.

A Disputed Doctrine

While the clarity of Scripture may seem, well, clear to certain Christians, it is held in suspicion by many others. The typical objections can be grouped under three headings.

The mystical objection. According to this view—often a mood or an overreaction more than a formal school of thought—God is so transcendent that he cannot be talked about meaningfully with words. On a popular level this is usually communicated as a humble attempt to rescue God from all our man-made theologizing. The Christian faith, it is said, is utterly mysterious. It's about things that can't be put into words. You can't put God in a box, after all. Truth cannot be captured in words or propositions. At the very least, this means we should be radically uncertain about our interpretations of Scripture. At the most, it suggests Scripture itself is nothing more than a feeble attempt to describe the mysteries of faith using the imperfections of human language.

The Catholic objection. Protestants and Catholics have historically held to the same understanding of inspiration and inerrancy, but they have differed when it comes to some of the attributes of Scripture. Catholic theologians argue that the Bible as a whole is not sufficiently clear in itself. Scripture is, in some parts, incomplete and needs to be explained and augmented by tradition. On our own, therefore, we are apt to misunderstand and misapply the Scriptures. We need someone or something to offer an authoritative and binding interpretation. The task of giving an "authentic interpretation" of the word of God has been given to the magisterium, that is, to the pope and to the bishops in communion with him.[1]

The pluralism objection. This objection is based on an assessment of our present interpretative predicament. If the Bible is so clear, the argument goes, then why can't Christians agree on what it means? Why are there so many denominations? Why are there so many Christian books with four views of this and five views of that? People claim to know what the Bible means, but how can it be so clear if the church used the Bible to justify slavery or the crusades or a flat earth or a geocentric view of the universe? In the

---

[1] *Catechism of the Catholic Church*, 2nd ed., 1997, part 1, section 1, chapter 2, article 2, III [#85, 100].

end, the argument is not so much about whether a particular interpretation *is* right or wrong. The pluralism objection questions the very idea that any of us has sufficient grounds to *know* whether an interpretation is right or wrong.

Rather than responding to each specific objection point by point, I'd like to take a broader approach and see what the Bible says about its own clarity. By walking through the Scriptures, and then drawing out some of the implications of what we find, I think our initial definition can be supported and the various objections can be addressed. We'll start by looking at the passage that led off this chapter.

Near, Not Far

The book of Deuteronomy records the second giving of the law, just as the Israelites stand on the brink of entering the Promised Land (Deut. 1:1–8). Working backward, chapter 34 records the death of Moses, chapter 33 the final blessing of Moses, chapter 32 the Song of Moses, chapter 31 the selection of Joshua to succeed Moses, and chapters 1–30 constitute a long sermon and covenant renewal ceremony spoken by the Lord through the mouth of Moses. Chapters 29 and 30, quite logically, serve as the climactic conclusion to Moses's sermon. Zooming in a bit further, we find that Deuteronomy 30:11–20 is the final exhortation in this lengthy oration. Moses is imploring the people to choose life, instead of death, by keeping the commandments and statutes of the Lord (vv. 15–20). That's the point of all that Moses has laid out in chapters 1–30. But in order to make this charge effective, Moses must demonstrate that he is not asking the people to do something that is impossible. So just before the exhortation in verses 15–20, Moses reassures the people in verses 11–14 that God's word is not beyond them.

Ironically enough, this passage about the simplicity of God's word is not the easiest to understand. At first glance, it seems to fly in the face of Paul's statements about the law and our inability to keep it. How can Moses say the commandment "is not too hard for you" (v. 11) and that "you can do it" (v. 14) if "none is righteous, no, not one" (Rom. 3:10)? I thought the law was given precisely because we couldn't keep it (see Gal. 3:19–22). And, of course, that *is* true about the law as a means of our own deliverance. But Moses is not talking about law-keeping as self-justification. He is speaking to a people already saved from Egypt, already graciously set free, already delivered apart from any law-keeping. He's exhorting them to live as God's chosen, redeemed, free people. And so Moses reassures them that the word of God can be *understood* and *obeyed*—not perfectly and not meritoriously, but in a way that pleases the God who has already graciously saved them. When you think of it, it's not any different from Jesus telling his disciples to obey everything he commanded them (Matt. 28:20) or John declaring that "his commandments are not burdensome" (1 John 5:3).

The picture of the word of God in Deuteronomy 30:11–14 is of something that can be comprehended clearly. "They could never plead in excuse of their disobedience," explains Matthew Henry, "that God had enjoined them that which was either unintelligible or impracticable, impossible to be known or done."[2] You don't have to go to heaven to get God's

---

[2] Matthew Henry, *Commentary on the Whole Bible*, ed. Leslie F. Church (Grand Rapids, MI: Zondervan, 1961), 200. See also "The Pleasure of God and the Possibility of Godliness," chapter 5 in my book *The Hole in Our Holiness* (Wheaton, IL: Crossway, 2012).

word (v. 12). You don't have to cross an ocean to find it (v. 13). God's word is not inaccessible or esoteric. As Calvin puts it, "God does not propound to us obscure enigmas to keep our minds in suspense, and to torment us with difficulties, but teaches familiarly whatever is necessary, according to the capacity, and consequently the ignorance of the people."[3]

What God wanted from his people was not hidden far off in the sky or stored far away beyond the sea. The law can be on our lips. It can be taught to our children (Deut. 6:7). God's revealed will does not require searching out and solving the mysteries of the universe (29:29). The word of God is near, not far, right in front of you, ready to be understood and obeyed.

Confirmation Basis

What Deuteronomy teaches about the clarity of God's word is confirmed throughout the rest of the Bible. In the Psalms, for example, the psalmist compares God's word to light. The word is a lamp to our feet and a light to our path (Ps. 119:105). The unfolding of his words gives light and imparts understanding to the simple (v. 130). The law makes wise the simple and enlightens the eyes (19:7–8). Since God is light (1 John 1:5), we would expect his word also to be clear and bright. After all, God communicates to reveal, not to obscure.

When the book of the law was rediscovered in Josiah's day, the people read it, understood it, and knew what they had to do in response (2 Kings 22–23). The meaning of the text was not lost on them, even after the passage of many years.

---

[3] John Calvin, *Calvin's Commentaries, Volume 2*, trans. Charles William Bingham (Grand Rapids, MI: Baker, 1993), 412.

What point would there be in uttering threats and promises to a hurting, scared, lawless, desperate people unless it was assumed that all those threats and promises could be understood, at least enough for the people to respond in faith and repentance? The presence of the prophets, God's "covenant attorneys," makes sense only on the assumption that they had a right to press home the points of the law that the people should have known and followed but were ignoring. In fact, the warp and woof of the entire Old Testament assumes that holy words and holy texts are adequate vehicles for the transmission of God's intentions and desires. That's why Nehemiah can tell us that Ezra and the priests "read from the book, from the Law of God, clearly, and they gave the sense, so that the people understood the reading" (Neh. 8:8): not just their *interpretation*, but the *meaning* of God's word.

This same approach to Scripture was shared by Jesus and the apostles. Dozens of times Jesus appealed to a text from the Old Testament, thinking that such an appeal settled the matter. This implies that Jesus believed not only that the Old Testament was authoritative, but that it had a fixed meaning which people should have been able to recognize. Jesus often referred to the Scriptures as evidence for the veracity of his teaching (see Matt. 21:42–44; Mark 10:4–9; John 10:34–35). Other times he chided the Jewish establishment for not conforming to the word of God (Matt. 21:13; Mark 7:6–13). "Go and learn what this means, 'I desire mercy, and not sacrifice,'" Jesus said on one occasion (Matt. 9:13), suggesting that they should have understood how this verse from Hosea applied to the "scandal" of his eating with tax collectors and sinners. Six times Jesus asks, "Have you not read . . . ," suggesting that if his opponents had known the Scriptures better, they would not be making the mistake they were making. Jesus approached God's written revelation as if it could be known and understood. And the apostles did the same, quoting from the Scriptures, reasoning from them, alluding to them, and finding the fulfillment of them, all with the assumption that these texts had a correct meaning and the apostles were in possession of it.

The Clarity Imperative

The clarity of Scripture is one of those doctrines that you don't really miss until it's gone. It's constantly being undermined by well-meaning (and sometimes not so well-meaning) Christians who think it's the better part of piety to question the intelligibility of verbal revelation. The challenges to the clarity of Scripture start out small. They sound humble and practical at first. But in the end, if we lose this attribute of Scripture—so plainly taught, if not simply assumed, in the pages of the Bible—we lose some of the most precious and hard-fought truths the church must have if it is to grow and flourish. There is a lot at stake with this doctrine.

First, the gift of human language is at stake. It sounds humble to say, "We can't put God in a box. We can't define him with human language. If we could define him with our words, then he wouldn't be God anymore. Scripture simply gives us one inspired record of human beings trying to describe mysteries that are beyond mere words and language." That sounds nice, even noble. But there are several hidden assumptions in a soliloquy like that:

- If God cannot be described with words exhaustively, then he cannot be described at all truthfully.

- Scripture is not God revealing himself to us, but the record of humans trying to understand God.
- Human language is so irredeemably flawed, inaccurate, and impotent as to render it an unusable means of divine communication.

Each of these assumptions is mistaken. Just because God cannot be known exhaustively, that does not mean he cannot be known at all. Theologians have long distinguished between archetypal knowledge (that which God has of himself) and ectypal knowledge (that which we have by virtue of his self-revelation). And nowhere do Jesus or the apostles ever treat the Old Testament as human reflections on the divine. It is instead the voice of the Holy Spirit (Acts 4:25; Heb. 3:7) and God's own breath (2 Tim. 3:16).

More to the point, human language, however imperfect and imprecise at times, is best seen as a divine gift. God is the first one in the universe to speak. To be more precise, his speech calls the universe into being (Heb. 11:3). Then he comes to Adam with words, expecting the image-bearer to understand what he communicates and obey his statutes. And who is it that first challenges the clarity of verbal revelation? It is the Serpent, challenging whether God has really spoken what Adam and Eve heard him say (Gen. 3:1).

God is the divine speaker antecedent to all human speaking. The facility for language is part of the gift God gives to us of himself. It is one thing to suggest that God cannot be known absolutely or contained in any verbal system. It's appropriate to admit that language can be used deceitfully and is subject to ambiguity. But if we are created in the image of God, then it stands to reason that we are fit conversation partners for the God who began the universe by speaking. Human language is a divinely created means whereby God, from the very beginning, intended to make himself and his ways known.

Second, the gift of human freedom is at stake. The Protestant doctrine of perspicuity is one of the foundations for religious liberty in the West. Implicit in the affirmation of Scripture's clarity is the recognition that individuals have the responsibility and the ability to interpret Scripture for themselves: Not apart from community, or without attention to history and tradition and scholarship. But in the final analysis, the doctrine of perspicuity means that I should not be forced to go against my own conscience. Only Jesus Christ, speaking through the word, is Lord of the conscience.

Of course, this most Protestant of doctrines has opened a door to all sorts of problems—factions, eccentric interpretations, rampant individualism, and the like. But despite these dangers, the freedom that perspicuity protects is worth the cost. Herman Bavinck explains:

> On balance, however, the disadvantages do not outweigh the advantages. For the denial of the clarity of Scripture carries with it the subjection of the layperson to the priest, or a person's conscience to the church. The freedom of religion and the human conscience, of the church and theology, stands and falls with the perspicuity of Scripture. It alone is able to maintain the freedom of the Christian; it is the origin and guarantee of religious liberty as well as of our political freedoms. Even a freedom that cannot be obtained and enjoyed aside from the

dangers of licentiousness and caprice is still always so
to be preferred over a tyranny that suppresses liberty.[4]

The biblical doctrine of perspicuity can be abused. But
a raft of bad interpretations and the sometimes free-for-all
of Protestantism is still worth the price of reading the Bible
for ourselves according to our God-given (and imperfect) con-
sciences. Freedom of religious inquiry and expression would
not be possible without confidence in the clarity of Scripture.

Third, what God is like is at stake. The fantastic work
by D. A. Carson, *The Gagging of God*,[5] is aptly named. At
the heart of the postmodern skepticism about knowing God
is an inferior conception of what God is like. The question
is not whether we are haughty enough to think we have
peered into the recesses of eternity and understand God om-
nisciently. The question is whether God is the sort of God
who is willing to communicate with his creatures and able to
do so effectively. Can God speak? Or is he gagged?

You may have come across the little story about the six
blind men and the elephant. There are six blind men touch-
ing an elephant, trying to determine what it is they feel. One
man touches the belly of the animal and thinks it's a wall.
Another grabs his ear and thinks it's a fan. Another thinks
his tail is a rope. On they go, each grabbing a part of the
elephant without any one of them knowing what it is they
really feel. The point of story? We are all blind men when
it comes to God. We know a part of him, but we don't really
know who he is. No one is more right than anyone else. We

[4] Herman Bavinck, *Reformed Dogmatics, Volume 1: Prolegomena*, ed. John Bolt, trans. John Vriend
(Grand Rapids, MI: Baker Academic, 2003), 479.

[5] D. A. Carson, *The Gagging of God: Christianity Confronts Pluralism* (Grand Rapids, MI: Zondervan, 1996).

are all just grasping in the dark, thinking we know more than we do.

But of course there are two enormous problems with the analogy. For starters, the whole story is told from the vantage point of someone who clearly knows that the elephant is an elephant. For the story to make its point, the narrator has to have clear and accurate knowledge of the elephant. The second flaw is even more serious. The story is a perfectly good description of human inability in matters of the divine. We are blind and unable to know God by our own devices. But the story never considers this paradigm-shattering question: What if the elephant talks? What if he tells the blind men, "That wall-like structure is my side. That fan is really my ear. And that's not a rope; it's a tail." If the elephant were to say all this, would the six blind men be considered humble for ignoring his word?

We must not separate epistemology (that is, our theory of what we know and how we can know it) from the rest of theology. These high-sounding debates about perspicuity and hermeneutics really have to do with the character of God. Is God wise enough to make himself known? Is he good enough to make himself accessible? Is he gracious enough to communicate in ways that are understandable to the meek and lowly? Or does God give us commands we can't understand and a self-revelation that reveals more questions than answers?

Finally, whom God is for is at stake. The doctrine of the clarity of Scripture insists that even the simplest disciple can understand God's word and be saved. Without this doctrine, you have to wonder: Is the Bible only for pastors and priests? Can laypeople be trusted with the sacred Scriptures? Do you need to be a scholar to really understand God's word? Do you need a working knowledge of Greek and Hebrew, of Second Temple Judaism, of Greco-Roman customs, of ancient Near Eastern religion, or redaction criticism, source criticism, and form criticism? Is God a God of the smarty-pants only? As R. C. Sproul asks, "What kind of God would reveal his love and redemption in terms so technical and concepts so profound that only an elite corps of professional scholars could understand them?"[6]

William Tyndale (1494–1536) was often maligned and in danger for his efforts to translate the Bible into the common language of the people. On one occasion when in dispute with a "learned man," he replied, "If God spare my life [before] many years I will cause a boy that driveth the plough shall know more of scripture than thou dost."[7] That's confidence in the doctrine of the clarity of Scripture. And it cost Tyndale his life. He died by strangulation, and his corpse was burned in the city square. Fittingly, at the stake he cried out these last words with a loud voice: "Lord, open the King of England's eyes."[8] Yes, Lord, open our eyes to see the power and privilege we have to read the Scriptures in a language we can understand. Open our eyes to behold wonderful things in your law. Open our eyes to see the truth you have clearly laid before us. God has made it plain—to all of us—if only we have the eyes to see.

---

[6] Quoted in Mark D. Thompson, *A Clear and Present Word: The Clarity of Scripture* (Downers Grove, IL: InterVarsity Press, 2006), 79.

[7] David Daniell, *William Tyndale: A Biography* (New Haven, CT: Yale University Press, 1994), 79.

[8] Ibid., 383.

5

God's Word
Is Final

Now when they had passed through Amphipolis and Apollonia, they came to Thessalonica, where there was a synagogue of the Jews. And Paul went in, as was his custom, and on three Sabbath days he reasoned with them from the Scriptures, explaining and proving that it was necessary for the Christ to suffer and to rise from the dead, and saying, "This Jesus, whom I proclaim to you, is the Christ." And some of them were persuaded and joined Paul and Silas, as did a great many of the devout Greeks and not a few of the leading women. But the Jews were jealous, and taking some wicked men of the rabble, they formed a mob, set the city in an uproar, and attacked the house of Jason, seeking to bring them out to the crowd. And when they could not find them, they dragged Jason and some of the brothers before the city authorities, shouting, "These men who have turned the world upside down have come here also, and Jason has received them, and they are all acting against the decrees of Caesar, saying that there is another king, Jesus." And the people and the city authorities were disturbed when they heard these things. And when they had taken money as security from Jason and the rest, they let them go.

The brothers immediately sent Paul and Silas away by night to Berea, and when they arrived they went into the Jewish synagogue. Now these Jews were more noble than those in Thessalonica; they received the word with all eagerness, examining the Scriptures daily to see if these things were so. Many of them therefore believed, with not a few Greek women of high standing as well as men. But when the Jews from Thessalonica learned that the word of God was proclaimed by Paul at Berea also, they came there too, agitating and stirring up the crowds. Then the brothers immediately sent Paul off on his way to the sea, but Silas and Timothy remained there. Those who conducted Paul brought him as far as Athens, and after

receiving a command for Silas and Timothy to come to him as soon
as possible, they departed.

ACTS 17:1–15

These two episodes—one in Thessalonica and one in Berea—
have a lot in common. In both cities, Paul began his evange-
listic work in the synagogue (vv. 1, 10). On both occasions we
see the word proclaimed and examined and the use of reason
and persuasion (vv. 2, 3, 4, 11, 13). And in both instances the
general response was similar: controversy ensued because
some received the word (vv. 4, 12) while some hated it (vv. 5,
13). The mission ventures in Thessalonica and Berea were
similar to each other in several ways and much like Paul's
experience preaching the gospel in other Greco-Roman cities.

But not similar in every way. The comparisons above are
misleading in one respect. While the gospel proclamation
was controversial in both cities, the crowds were agitated in
Berea because Jews from *Thessalonica* had come to stir them
up. Even though the basic outline of events is the same, we
are clearly meant to see a contrast between the Thessalonian
and the Berean approaches to the word of God.

Theatrical Thessalonians

The Thessalonian attitude toward the truth of the gospel is
destructive, bordering on delirious. For starters, their judgment is clouded by personal prejudice. The Jews don't like
that Paul is popular (Acts 17:5). In fact, it's a good bet most
of the converts in Thessalonica were from paganism, not
from Judaism (1 Thess. 1:9). Paul's own people disregarded

his message because they thought he was too much of a big shot. Unfortunately, this sort of prejudice happens all the time. People will dismiss the word of God because the music in church is too loud or too old, or the church is too small or too big, or because the pastor dresses funny, or because they knew a mean Christian once, or because they don't want to be like their parents.

And sometimes we find a reason to reject the word of God because we aren't interested in doing what it says. As Aldous Huxley, the famous author of *Brave New World* who dabbled in eastern mysticism and LSD, once remarked,

> For myself, as, no doubt, for most of my contemporaries, the philosophy of meaninglessness was essentially an instrument of liberation. The liberation we desired was simultaneously liberation from a certain political and economic system and liberation from a certain system of morality. We objected to the morality because it interfered with our sexual freedom; we objected to the political and economic system because it was unjust.[1]

No doubt some people reject the gospel and the Bible because of genuine intellectual concerns, but just as often, I'm convinced, pride and personal prejudice are to blame. We don't like the people teaching the Bible, and we don't like what the Bible teaches. So we get our hearts dead set against the word of God, just as the Thessalonians did.

The Thessalonians were also blind to their own inconsistencies. Have you ever known someone to make the propositional statement, "I can't believe in a religion built on

---

[1] Aldous Huxley, in Robert S. Baker and James Sexton, eds., *Aldous Huxley: Complete Essays, Volume 4* (Lanham, MD: Ivan R. Dee, 2001), 369.

propositional truth," or to utter the intolerant sentiment, "I can't stand intolerant jerks"? A similar inconsistency is on display with the Thessalonians. They complain about the Christians who have rocked the boat and "turned the world upside down" (Acts 17:6). So what do they do? They form a mob, set the city in an uproar, and drag a man named Jason out of his house (vv. 5–6). They can't see the inconsistency of their charge against Paul and Silas. They are blind to their own sins and double standard. Just like the student who refuses to "go along with the crowd," so instead she dresses, talks, shops, thinks, and styles her hair like a thousand other "rebels." Or like the judgmental person who lambasts judgmentalism, or the leader who says, "Question authority" based on his own authority, or the person who pushes his libertine morality on everyone else because he's tired of everyone pushing their own morality. Some people reject God's word because they always spot in others what they would never see in themselves.

And when people are full of prejudice and blind to their own inconsistencies, they end up attacking people instead of advancing arguments. The Thessalonians resort to verbal abuse (v. 6), twisting the truth (v. 7), and physical assault (v. 5). This is a very diligent mob, walking forty-five miles over to Berea in an effort to turn that city against the disciples. They aren't interested in a reasoned consideration of Christian claims. They are interested in the utter destruction of a sect they've already concluded is dangerous and worthy of contempt. Some opponents of the word of God come by their objections honestly, but others have never stopped to search the Scriptures for themselves. They've already decided the Bible is antiscience, antiwoman, and antigay, without bothering to define those terms or investigate the Bible with calm reason and an open mind.

Better Bereans

The Jews in Berea, by contrast, were more noble than their counterparts in Thessalonica. They were eager to hear the word and persistent in studying the Scriptures (v. 11). Daily they examined the Scriptures to see if Paul's word could be supported by God's word. They were looking into things, testing what they heard, diligent to discern what was the truth.

When I speak at different conferences and churches, I'm often surprised how few people bother to look at their Bibles when I'm speaking. Be it laziness, forgetfulness, or something else, it's not a good habit. I have no authority in myself. I don't want people to just take my word for it. God's people should be testing everything against God's word. Whether we are the ones teaching or listening, we need to have our Bibles open like the Bereans.

Every day the Bereans searched the Scriptures to see if Paul's gospel had divine authority. And they confirmed that what they heard was true to Scripture, and "therefore [they] believed" (v. 12). The Bereans were more noble than the Thessalonians because they were utterly submissive to the Scriptures. They would accept something new—if it could be supported in the Scriptures. They would believe something controversial—if it was based in Scripture. They were willing to follow Christ for the rest of their lives, provided they were, in the process, following the Scriptures.

This passage perfectly demonstrates what it means to affirm the authority of the Bible. When it says the Bereans were "examining the Scriptures daily to see if these things were so" (v. 11), the implication is that if the Scripture said it, they would believe it. And if they couldn't find Paul's teaching confirmed in and consistent with the Scripture, they would reject Paul's teaching. The written word of God was their authority. It had the last word. It was the final word, after which no other word would be necessary, and contrary to which no other word would be believed.

A Question of Authority

If you've ever wondered why different professing Christians come to such wildly different theological conclusions, at least a part of the answer—the biggest part, in fact—has to do with the question of authority. The three main branches of Christianity in the West—traditional Roman Catholic, liberal Protestant, and evangelical—do not agree on how to adjudicate competing truth claims. We don't answer the question "What is our ultimate authority?" in the same way. Every Christian acknowledges that in some sense our theology and ethics must "accord with Scripture." But when push comes to shove in theological wrangling, to whom or what do we appeal to make our closing arguments?

See if you can spot the differences in these three statements on Scripture and authority, representing different branches of contemporary Western Christianity.

The first is from Peter Kreeft, a fine writer and winsome Roman Catholic:

> The Church gives us her Tradition like a mother giving a child hand-me-down clothing that has already been worn by many older sisters and brothers. But unlike any

earthly clothing, this clothing is indestructible because it is not made of wool or cotton but truth. It was invented by God, not man. Sacred Tradition (capital "T") must be distinguished from all human traditions (small "t").

Sacred Tradition is part of "the deposit of faith", which also includes Sacred Scripture. It is comprised of the Church's data, given to her by her Lord.[2]

The second statement is from Gary Dorrien, the foremost expert on American liberal theology and himself a liberal Protestant:

The essential idea of liberal theology is that all claims to truth, in theology as in other disciplines, must be made on the basis of reason and experience, not by appeal to external authority. Christian scripture may be recognized as spiritually authoritative within Christian experience, but its word does not settle or establish truth claims about matters of fact.[3]

And finally, here's a third statement, from the Westminster Confession of Faith, which on this point is representative of broader evangelicalism:

The supreme judge by which all controversies of religion are to be determined, and all decrees of councils, opinions of ancient writers, doctrines of men, and private spirits, are to be examined and in whose sentence we are to rest, can be no other but the Holy Spirit speaking in the Scripture. (WCF 1.10)

---

[2] Peter Kreeft, *Catholic Christianity: A Complete Catechism of Catholic Church Beliefs Based on the Catechism of the Catholic Church* (San Francisco: Ignatius, 2001), 18.

[3] Gary Dorrien, *The Making of American Liberal Theology: Idealism, Realism, and Modernity, 1900–1950* (Louisville: Westminster John Knox, 2003), 1.

The differences in these statements are striking. For Kreeft, church tradition is a final authority, on par with Scripture. For Dorrien, Scripture must align with reason and experience. But for Westminster, the word of God stands outside and over and above the church and all human opinion. Whatever else we may disagree on as Catholics, liberals, and evangelicals, we should at least agree that it is our view of Scripture and authority that divides us.

All religion rests on authority. In fact, every academic discipline and every sphere of human inquiry rests on authority. Whether we realize it or not, we all give someone or something the last word—our parents, our culture, our community, our feelings, the government, peer-reviewed journals, opinion polls, impressions, or a holy book. We all have someone or something that we turn to as the final arbiter of truth claims. For Christians, this authority is the Scriptures of the Old and New Testaments. Of course, we can misunderstand and misapply the word of God. But when interpreted correctly—paying attention to the original context, considering the literary genre, thinking through authorial intent—the Bible is never wrong in what it affirms and must never be marginalized as anything less than the last word on everything it teaches.

Two Books, One Final Authority

God reveals himself to us in two ways: through the universe we can see, and through the Scripture we can hear and read. General revelation is God's self-disclosure through the created world. Special revelation is God's self-disclosure through the spoken and written words of divinely inspired messengers. Both means of revelation are important, and both are taught in Scripture.

It has often been pointed out that because the revelation in both of these "Two Books" is from God, the two teach the same truth. "All truth is God's truth," as the saying goes. In the end there can be no conflict between what God reveals in Scripture and what he reveals in nature. If all the facts could be known perfectly, we would find that the Bible and science do not contradict each other. Christians have nothing to fear from rigorous scientific investigation.

And yet, if the Bible is our final authority—as it surely was for the Bereans—then we must be hesitant to scrub the Bible when it seems to contradict the "assured results of science." I sympathize with Christians who struggle to reconcile what they hear from scientists and what they see in the Bible about a particular issue. We should not be quick to dismiss these questions. It is possible to read the Bible wrongly. It is possible for the church to miss the mark for a long time. But every Christian should agree that if the Bible teaches one thing and scientific consensus teaches something else, we will not ditch the Bible. The Two Books are not separate, but they are unequal.

The Belgic Confession provides a standard definition of general and special revelation:

We know him [God] by two means:

First, by the creation, preservation, and government of the universe, since the universe is before our eyes like a beautiful book in which all creatures, great and small, are as letters to make us ponder the invisible things of God; his eternal power and his divinity, as the apostle

Paul says in Romans 1:20. All these things are enough to convict men and to leave them without excuse.

Second, he makes himself known to us more openly by his holy and divine Word, as much as we need in this life, for his glory and for the salvation of his own. (Article 2)[4]

Notice the difference between general and special revelation. The former gives us a sense of God's power and divine nature so that we are left without excuse. The latter reveals God "more openly" so that we might be saved. The doctrine of general and special revelation was never meant to make the Bible artificially conform to any other academic discipline. The heavens declare the glory of God, but the law of the Lord is perfect and the testimony of the Lord is sure (Ps. 19:1, 7). Jesus can illustrate with the lilies of the field (Matt. 6:28), but "it is written" can conquer the Devil (4:1–11).

I am not for a moment arguing for obscurantism when it comes to the hard questions concerning faith and science. Pastors who haven't had a science class since the tenth grade are often too cavalier with the tough issues raised by geology, biology, and genetics. But surely it is the mark of a Christian to believe everything the Bible teaches no matter who says it can't be so. Academic journals are not infallible, let alone high school textbooks or fifteen-second sound bites. As Christians we must always be willing to change our minds when we see that we have misread the Scriptures, but that is a far cry from setting aside the Scriptures because for the last five years—or fifty years or a hundred and fifty years— some scientists have informed us that we can't believe in

---

[4] *Ecumenical Creeds and Reformed Confessions* (Grand Rapids, MI: Faith Alive Christian Resources, 1987).

the historicity of Adam or that the universe was created out of nothing by the word of God. General revelation can show us there is a God and convict those who don't worship him rightly. But special revelation speaks more clearly, more openly, and more authoritatively. If Scripture gets the last word, we should never change a jot or tittle of the Holy Book merely because the book of nature—for a time and according to some voices—seems to suggest we should.

Believing In Order to Understand

Many thoughtful Christians, who affirm the inerrancy and final authority of Scripture, and who study the Bible long enough and hard enough, eventually stumble upon problems in the biblical text that don't afford simple solutions. There are dates that are hard to reconcile and numbers that don't seem to fit. There are apparent discrepancies that are not easily harmonized and questions without easy answers. These may seem strange admissions in a chapter on the authority of Scripture, but Christians should not be afraid to admit what we see. If Peter found some things in Paul's letters "hard to understand" (2 Pet. 3:16), we too are bound to be perplexed now and then.

But given everything we have already seen about a biblical doctrine of Scripture, we have no reason to be intimidated by difficulties and apparent discrepancies in the Bible. Many of them are easily explained. Most of the rest of them have good, plausible solutions. And for the few humdingers that are left, there are possible explanations, even if we aren't sure that we've found the right one yet. Our confidence in the Bible is not an irrational confidence. The findings of history, archaeology, and textual criticism give us many reasons to trust the Old and New Testaments. But more than all the apologetic evidence—and it can be found by anyone who cares to read the best books out there—we have the testimony of God himself. The Bible is God's book, a fact we are reminded of frequently in the book. Consequently, to trust completely in the Bible is to trust in the character and assurances of God more than we trust in our own ability to reason and explain.

Again, J. I. Packer puts it perfectly. This long paragraph is worth reading slowly:

> God, then, does not profess to answer in Scripture all the questions that we, in our boundless curiosity, would like to ask about Scripture. He tells us merely as much as He sees we need to know as a basis for our life of faith. And He leaves unsolved some of the problems raised by what He tells us, in order to teach us a humble trust in His veracity. The question, therefore, that we must ask ourselves when faced with these puzzles is not, is it reasonable to imagine that this is so? but, is it reasonable to accept God's assurance that this is so? Is it reasonable to take God's word and believe that He has spoken the truth, even though I cannot fully comprehend what He has said? The question carries its own answer. We should not abandon faith in anything God has taught us merely because we cannot solve all the problems which it raises. Our own intellectual competence is not the test and measure of divine truth. It is not for us to stop believing because we lack understanding, but to believe in order that we may understand.[5]

---

[5] J. I. Packer, *"Fundamentalism" and the Word of God* (Grand Rapids, MI: Eerdmans, 1958), 109.

Did the Bereans ever have questions about the Scriptures that they couldn't answer? Perhaps. There is no way to know for sure. What we do know is that they were commended for the singular virtue of giving Scripture the last word. They tested everything against the Scriptures because they dared not accept what Scripture denied or miss what Scripture affirmed. They approached their Bibles with a reverence fitting for God alone. Which makes sense, because ultimately, we commit ourselves to the authority of the word of God because the God whose word it is informs us that we can and tells us that we must.

6

God's Word
Is Necessary

Yet among the mature we do impart wisdom, although it is not a wisdom of this age or of the rulers of this age, who are doomed to pass away. But we impart a secret and hidden wisdom of God, which God decreed before the ages for our glory. None of the rulers of this age understood this, for if they had, they would not have crucified the Lord of glory. But, as it is written,

> "What no eye had seen, nor ear heard,
>   nor the heart of man imagined,
> what God has prepared for those who love him"—

these things God has revealed to us through the Spirit. For the Spirit searches everything, even the depths of God. For who knows a person's thoughts except the spirit of that person, which is in him? So also no one comprehends the thoughts of God except the Spirit of God. Now we have received not the spirit of the world, but the Spirit who is from God, that we might understand the things freely given us by God. And we impart this in words not taught by human wisdom but taught by the Spirit, interpreting spiritual truths to those who are spiritual.

1 CORINTHIANS 2:6-13

Most of us, deep down, want the same things out of life. Of course, I'm talking about ultimate things, not immediate things. On the immediate level, people have a wide variety of desires. Some people like to travel. Some people like fine dining. Some people prefer indoor plumbing and a comfortable bed. And other people like camping. There are a million different tastes, interests, and hobbies. But if we get to the level of the heart, I think people all around the world generally want the same things: We want purpose. We want to be happy. We want to know we are okay. We want to be a part of something bigger than ourselves. We want to be known by someone bigger than ourselves. We want to live forever.

And if you dig around in those desires, you'll find that most people are waiting for some word from somewhere so that they can finally know this good life. They want a law or a list that will tell them steps to take to get there. They want their teacher to say, "You've passed," or their parents to say, "I love you." They want to get a call from their dream job or their dream date. They want to hear good news about their retirement fund or their health or their kids. Many of them are listening intently to hear from the most sacred voice they know: their own. And some are desperate to hear from God.

The doctrine of the necessity of Scripture reminds us of our predicament: the One we need to know most cannot be discovered on our own. And it assures us of a solution: this same ineffable One has made himself known through his word. As the Westminster Confession of Faith explains, "Although the light of nature and the works of creation and providence do so far manifest the goodness, wisdom, and power of God, as to leave men inexcusable; yet are they not sufficient to give that knowledge of God, and of his will, which is necessary unto salvation." Holy Scripture, the Confession goes on to say, is therefore "most necessary" (WCF 1.1). The Scriptures are our spectacles (to use Calvin's phrase), the lenses through which we see God, the world, and ourselves rightly. We cannot truly know God, his will, or the way of salvation apart from the Bible.

We need Scripture to live the truly good life. We need Scripture to live forever. "Lord, to whom shall we go? You have the words of eternal life" (John 6:68). There is no other book like the Bible. It reveals a different kind of wisdom, comes from a different source, and tells of a different love.

A Different Wisdom

Wisdom is one of the main themes in the opening chapters of 1 Corinthians. Writing amid a Greek culture that lauded fine-sounding philosophers and fancy orators as the rock stars of their day, Paul takes great pains to differentiate the gospel from that kind of wisdom. If you are looking for wisdom in sophisticated speech and powerful rhetoric, Paul says, you'll not find it in the preaching of the cross (1 Cor. 1:18–25). You'll not find it in my sermons (2:1–5). And you'll not find it in many of yourselves (1:26–31).

The gospel is wisdom for the mature (2:6), but it has nothing to do with the "wisdom" this world longs to see. God's wisdom is not of this age (v. 6a). It doesn't belong to this earthly realm or this "not yet" moment in redemptive history. God's wisdom is not of the *rulers* of this age (v. 6b). It has nothing in common with scheming powerbrokers or the cunning devices of the Evil One (cf. 2 Cor. 4:4; 10:4–6). God's wisdom is unique. It is not immediately obvious to all or universally appreciated by all (1 Cor. 2:7).

We can get very frustrated when people don't see what we see, when good arguments from Scripture don't seem to carry the day. But we should not be surprised. God's wisdom is a secret and hidden wisdom. This doesn't mean we must cross the sea or climb into the heavens to find the wisdom of God. It means God must speak to us if we are to be truly wise. All truth may be God's truth, but all *saving* truth is *revealed* truth.

The word of the world is not like the word of God. One is new and now. The other is ancient and everlasting. One is fleeting ("doomed to pass away"; 1 Cor. 2:6) while the other is fixed and firm ("decreed before the ages"; v. 7). If we want the "wisdom" of passing fashions, impressive brains, and talented people, then we can look to the world. But if we want—and if we *need*—a wisdom that is beyond us, that is outside of us, that will never fail us, we must look into the things that "God has revealed to us through the Spirit" (v. 10).

A Different Source

So where do we go to learn the things God has revealed? Do we look to the trees? What about the inner light? How about community standards? Maybe human reason and experience? The clear testimony of 1 Corinthians is that only God can tell us about God. Just as the spirit of a person discloses the thoughts and feelings and intentions of that person, so also no one can make known the thoughts of God except the Spirit of God (1 Cor. 2:11). The only Being knowledgeable enough, wise enough, and skillful enough to reveal God to you is God himself.

Which raises an interesting question: isn't Paul really talking about the inner working of the Spirit and not the necessity of the Scriptures? You might be thinking to yourself, "I agree completely. We need God to tell us about God.

I can't know the truth unless God reveals it to me. And God speaks to me through the still small voice in my heart. When I look deep inside myself, that's where I hear from God. We receive the Spirit of God, who speaks to our spirit, telling us the things we can learn only from God."

Sounds plausible, but is that Paul's point? The "we" in 1 Corinthians 2:12 ("we have received . . . the Spirit [of] God") does not refer to all the Corinthians or to all of us, but to Paul and his companions. The contrast starts in verses 1–5 with Paul's "I" and then transitions to the "we" who imparted to the Corinthians "a secret and hidden wisdom of God" (v. 7). Paul is clearly thinking of "you Corinthians" and "we who have ministered the gospel to you" (see 3:9). So while it's true that every believer receives the Spirit and each of us needs the Spirit of God to illuminate the word of God, Paul is speaking here of the unique apostolic deposit of truth he has received and has passed on to the Corinthians. This is precisely what Jesus promised would happen (John 16:12–15), and it is how the apostles understood their teaching: not as the word of man but as the word of God (1 Thess. 2:13; cf. Rev. 1:1–2). Nothing in 1 Corinthians 2 suggests that the real way to hear from God is to seek out the bewildering ruminations of the self. Already in Corinth—Paul's most "charismatic" congregation—we see there is an objective standard of truth which supersedes private impressions or experience (1 Cor. 14:37–38; 15:1–4).

True, for a time the early church existed without the completed New Testament. But even then, their life and doctrine were in submission to the Scriptures they already had. And the new revelation being placed alongside the Old Testament had been carefully scrutinized as coming from the apostolic band (Eph. 2:20) and adhering to the apostolic gospel (Gal. 1:8). "Naturally, as long as the apostles were alive and visited the churches," Bavinck writes, "no distinction was made between their spoken and their written word. Tradition and Scripture were still unified. But when the first period was past and time-distance from the apostles grew greater, their writings became more important, and the necessity of the writings gradually intensified. The necessity of Holy Scripture, in fact, is not a stable but an ever-increasing attribute."[1] Paul knew the Corinthians needed the wisdom of God that could come only from the Spirit of God, and he wrote to them this word with the understanding that he had uniquely received the Spirit whereby he could proclaim to them the truth of the gospel.

People talk about "spirituality" as if it were generated by concentrated attention to the inner workings of the human soul. But true spirituality is not something found within us. It is something outside of us, created by the agency of God's transcendent Holy Spirit. We need the Spirit who is from God if we are to understand the things of God (1 Cor. 2:12). And where do we go to hear from God's Spirit? To those who were entrusted to be the very mouthpiece of the Spirit (2:9–13), to those who wrote the very oracles of God (Rom. 3:2), to those who have written down what God himself has breathed out (2 Tim. 3:16). So this is the necessity of Scripture in a nutshell: *We need the revelation of God to know God, and the only sure, saving, final, perfect revelation of God is found in Scripture.*

---

[1] Herman Bavinck, *Reformed Dogmatics, Volume 1: Prolegomena*, ed. John Bolt, trans. John Vriend (Grand Rapids, MI: Baker Academic, 2003), 470.

A Different Love

It may seem like there is nothing left to say about the necessity of Scripture, but that would be to miss the heart of Paul's argument. The reason for revelation is that we might know God's mercy and be saved. The uniqueness of Scripture is found not just in its wisdom or even in its divine origin. What makes the Bible utterly unlike any other book—religious or otherwise—is the unsurpassed grace we encounter in its pages. We need Scripture because without it we cannot know the love of God.

Our God speaks, and he speaks not simply to be heard and not merely to pass along information. He speaks so that we can begin to know the unknowable and fathom the unfathomable (1 Cor. 2:9; cf. Isa. 48:8). You may think you've seen it all, and you've heard it all, and you've experienced everything there is to experience. But you haven't seen or heard or imagined what the God of love has prepared for those who love him (1 Cor. 2:9). This is the good news of the cross. This is the good news for the forgiven and redeemed. And this is the good news you won't find anywhere else but in the word of God.

Only by the Spirit working through the word can we truly become spiritual. When we hear the word "spiritual," we may think of being quiet and contemplative, or demonstrative in worship, or spontaneous, or full of God-language, or especially fond of praise music. These are what Jonathan Edwards would call "non-signs."[2] They don't prove anything one way or the other. They can be fine characteristics, but on their own they certainly don't make you spiritual, not

---

[2] Jonathan Edwards, *The Works of Jonathan Edwards, Volume 2: Religious Affections*, ed. John E. Smith (New Haven, CT: Yale University Press, 1959), 127–190.

by the Bible's definition. The spiritual person understands spiritual truths (1 Cor. 2:13), whereas the natural (unspiritual) person does not accept the things of the Spirit of God, "for they are folly to him" (v. 14). And what are the things of the Spirit that the unspiritual cannot understand? Given the context, Paul is clearly referring to the crucifixion of the Lord of glory (v. 8). The spiritual person is the one who accepts the message of the cross (1:18–24). No matter how much you like angels or how much you pray or how eager you are to meditate or how much you are into yoga or how much you believe in miracles, if you do not understand, cherish, and embrace the cross, you are not a spiritual person. The spiritual person discerns spiritual things, starting with the substitutionary sacrifice of Christ for the sins of the world. Only by embracing this good news can we be wise. Only through this good news can we be forgiven. Only by listening to the Spirit speaking through the Scriptures can we know the love of God and be truly spiritual.

A Fantastic Four

It is worth taking a moment at the end of this chapter to consider what a difference these four attributes of Scripture make for everyday life and godliness. Counselors can counsel meaningfully because Scripture is sufficient. Bible study leaders can lead confidently because Scripture is clear. Preachers can preach with boldness because their biblical text is authoritative. And evangelists can evangelize with urgency because the Scripture is necessary.

These doctrines are eminently practical. If the Bible is everything we've seen, then why wouldn't we read it, study it, memorize it, and teach it to others? Why would we build our churches on the shallow soil of pragmatic philosophy? Why would we counsel with the leftovers of worldly wisdom? Why would we look first to the beauty of mountains or to the echo chamber of the self in our moments of deepest pain and crisis? Why would we infuse our worship services with so little Scripture? Why would we sing songs bereft of biblical substance? Why would we prostrate the word of God to even the smartest-sounding words of men?

God's word is final. God's word is understandable. God's word is necessary. God's word is enough. In every age, Christians will do battle wherever these attributes of Scripture are threatened and assaulted. But more importantly, on every *day* we will have to fight the fight of faith to really believe everything we know the Bible says about itself and, even more challenging, to live accordingly.

7

Christ's
Unbreakable Bible

If he called them gods to whom the word of God came—and Scripture
cannot be broken—do you say of him whom the Father consecrated
and sent into the world, "You are blaspheming," because I said, "I am
the Son of God"?

JOHN 10:35–36

At the heart of this chapter stands one question. It is a
simple question and a crucial question, one that must un-
deniably shape and set the agenda for our doctrine of Scripture. The question is this: What did Jesus believe about the
Bible?

If you are a Christian, by definition you ought to believe
what Jesus teaches. He is the Son of God. He is our Savior
and Lord. We must follow his example, obey his commands,
and embrace whatever understanding of Scripture he taught
and assumed. Surely this means we are wise to believe about
the Scriptures whatever Jesus believed about the Scriptures.

And if you are not a Christian, I imagine you still value
what Jesus said. Virtually all people, even people of other
religions, consider Jesus to be an important teacher. At the
very least, they believe that he was a noble man and a great
prophet. So if you are investigating Christianity or trying to

figure out not only what Christians believe but the foundation for everything they believe, this is one of the best places
to start: figure out what Jesus believed about the Bible.

We may not think of Jesus having a Bible. And granted,
he didn't have a King James Bible in his home somewhere.
James wasn't the king, and people didn't have books. But
they had scrolls, not usually in their homes but in the syna-
gogues. These sacred scrolls were among the most prized
possession in any community. Jewish worship focused on the
reading and explaining of these writings. Jesus, like every
first-century Jew, was very familiar with the Hebrew Scriptures, what we would call the Old Testament.

And so, again, the question I want to ask is, what was
Jesus's doctrine of Scripture? In this chapter, I'm not asking how Jesus *interpreted* the Bible or *fulfilled* the Bible,
or what he *taught from* the Bible. I'm addressing only the
simple, absolutely crucial question: what did Jesus believe
about his Bible? Unless we dare say Jesus was mistaken or
too cowardly to communicate all that he wanted to say about
the Scriptures, we must conclude that whatever the perfect
Son of God believed about the sacred writings, we should
believe the same. There should be nothing controversial at
all in affirming that Christ's doctrine of Scripture should be
our doctrine of Scripture.

And what was his doctrine of Scripture? To find out, let's
start in John's Gospel and then look at several passages in
Matthew.

Unbound and Unbroken

Jesus's response in John 10:35–36 is one of the most important things he ever said. And also one of the most confusing. Understanding the context will help.

The Jews wanted to stone Jesus (v. 31) because he, as a man, dared to make himself equal to God (v. 33). In response to this charge Jesus quotes from Psalm 82. He appeals to Scripture ("Law" [John 10:34] in this case being interchangeable with "Scripture" [v. 35]) to defend himself against the charge of blasphemy. The Jews were upset that he referred to himself as the "Son of God," so Jesus reminds them that in their Scriptures the word "gods" (*elohim*) was used in reference to wicked kings (or judges, or magistrates, or some governing authority). The use of "gods" in Psalm 82:6 seems troubling to us, but the psalmist, who is speaking for God at this point, is probably using a bit of sarcasm: "Look, I know you are so important that you are gods among men, but you will die like all other men." Jesus isn't trying to prove his divinity from this curious reference in Psalm 82. He's trying to puncture the pretensions of his adversaries: "You are so hung up on the word 'God,' but right here in the Scriptures these men were called 'gods.' You'll have to do better than that, to prosecute me merely because of a title."

The important part of Jesus's argument (for our considerations) is his offhanded comment that "Scripture cannot be broken" (John 10:35). Here's Jesus defending himself, and he's not making his point from the Torah or from one of the loftiest passages in Isaiah. He's making his case from one word in an obscure psalm. And yet he doesn't have to prove to anyone that Psalm 82 is authoritative. Jesus doesn't try to convince his opponents that "Scripture cannot be broken." He merely asserts that truth as a common ground they can all agree on. For Jesus, anything from Scripture, down to the individual words and the least-heralded passages, possessed unquestioned authority. "According to His infallible estimate," Robert Watts once remarked about Jesus, "it was sufficient proof of the infallibility of any sentence, or clause of a sentence, or phrase of a clause, to show that it constituted a portion of what the Jews called . . . 'the Scripture.'"[1] The word for "broken" (*luo*) means to loose, release, dismiss, or dissolve. In John 10:35 *luo* carries the sense of breaking, nullifying, or invalidating. It's Jesus's way of affirming that no word of Scripture can be falsified. No promise or threat can fall short of fulfillment. No statement can be found erroneous. Just like his Jewish audience, Jesus believed Scripture was the word of God, and as such, it would be gross impiety to think that any word spoken by God, or committed to writing by God, might be an errant word, a wrong word, or a broken word.

Not an Iota, Not a Dot

The second passage we'll look at to get a picture of Jesus's doctrine of Scripture comes from Matthew 5:17–19:

> Do not think that I have come to abolish the Law or the Prophets; I have not come to abolish them but to fulfill them. For truly, I say to you, until heaven and earth pass away, not an iota, not a dot, will pass from the Law until all is accomplished. Therefore whoever relaxes one of the

---

[1] Robert Watts, *The Rule of Faith and the Doctrine of Inspiration: The Carey Lectures for 1884* (London: Hodder & Stoughton, 1885), 139.

least of these commandments and teaches others to do the same will be called least in the kingdom of heaven, but whoever does them and teaches them will be called great in the kingdom of heaven.

The same word used in John 10:35 (*luo*; break) is translated "relaxes" in Matthew 5:19. The point is largely the same. Jesus rebukes anyone who would set aside or weaken even the "least" of God's commandments. Jesus uses several terms interchangeably—"Law or the Prophets," "the Law," "these commandments"—suggesting that he is thinking not merely of Mosaic imperatives but of the entire word of God. And given his reference to "an iota" (the smallest letter in the Greek alphabet) and "a dot" (tiny graphical hooks or markings which distinguish similar Hebrew letters), we can be sure Jesus was thinking in particular of the *written* word of God. Not the least little speck of Scripture has been abolished by Christ's coming. Fulfilled, yes, and understood more fully in light of this coming, but never broken, loosed, or relaxed. The one who does treat the Scripture that way deserves to be least in the kingdom of heaven. We would be hard pressed to find a more comprehensive confidence in Scripture than Jesus expresses in this passage.

But, someone may ask, doesn't Jesus sometimes argue that the Old Testament was wrong? Doesn't he actually correct the Scriptures on a few occasions? It may look that way, but upon closer inspection we see that Christ never corrects a verse of Scripture when rightly interpreted and applied. For example, the claim is made that Jesus relaxed the requirements of the Sabbath, thus violating his own principle and tweaking Scripture to be less rigid. But actually Jesus *appealed* to Scripture—to the story of David and his men eating the bread of the Presence—to show that the Pharisees were imposing standards which violated the teaching of Scripture (Mark 2:23–28).

It's also said that Jesus abolished the law by declaring all food clean (Mark 7:19). But this is a perfect example of what Jesus meant by saying that he had come to fulfill the law. Jesus never questions the divine origin of the cleanliness rituals or the truthfulness of what such laws commanded. He does, however, teach that, as a deeper understanding of the command, they should come to Christ in obedience to find the cleansing and purity they need (vv. 18–23).

Similarly, some Christians maintain that Jesus disagreed with the Mosaic allowance for divorce and considered the Scriptures to be mistaken on this crucial point. But in reality, Jesus did not reject the command of Moses; he provided a better interpretation of it. Whereas the more liberal Jews were taking the Mosaic allowance to be a blank check for divorce on almost any grounds, Jesus brought them back to the true meaning of the text. Divorce was acceptable as a concession in those situations where sexual immorality had taken place (Matt. 19:3–9).

The most difficult example is Jesus's comments in Matthew 5:38 about the "eye for an eye" legislation in the Mosaic covenant. In all the rest of the "you have heard that it was said" statements in Matthew 5, Jesus references some piece of Pharisaic or scribal tradition, but here he quotes from the Old Testament itself. And yet once again we see that Jesus is not correcting Scripture itself, but the misapplication of it. The so-called *lex talionis* (law of retaliation) is mentioned several times in the Torah (Ex. 21:24; Lev. 24:20; Deut.

19:21). The law, as an administration of public justice, was meant to punish wrongdoers *and* protect the community. We tend to see the law as institutionalized cruelty and revenge. But it was actually meant to prohibit such vicious responses to criminal behavior. The "eye for an eye" principle forbade disproportionate penalties. While it prescribed a just punishment, it also proscribed *anything more than* an eye for an eye. It did not allow for vigilante justice or personal revenge, even though that's how many in Jesus's day understood the commandment. The Jewish leaders were misapplying a public law code and turning it into their personal right for retaliation. Jesus was right—and true to the biblical passage—to correct this misappropriation of the text.

Throughout the Sermon on the Mount, and especially in Matthew 5, Jesus tries to impress upon his audience the real meaning of Scripture. He does not want to correct Scripture. He wants to bring its full weight to bear on the human heart. He does not want the word of God circumvented by human tradition or specious reasoning. Instead, every speck of Scripture must be applied to every speck of Christian discipleship. "For Jesus," writes Donald Macleod, "jot-and-tittle loyalty to Scripture is neither legalistic nor evasive. . . . Jot-and-tittle fulfillment of the law means avoiding anger as well as homicide; lust as well as fornication; swearing as well as perjury. It means turning the other cheek, going the extra mile, and blowing no trumpets when we make donations to charity."[2] Jesus wants more of Scripture in our lives, not less.

This is exactly the point Jesus reiterates in Matthew 23:23, where he exhorts the people to keep "the weightier

---

[2] Donald Macleod, "Jesus and Scripture," in *The Trustworthiness of God: Perspectives on the Nature of Scripture*, ed. Paul Helm and Carl Trueman (Grand Rapids, MI: Eerdmans, 2002), 73.

matters of the law: justice and mercy and faithfulness," *without* neglecting the responsibility they have to tithe their mint, dill, and cumin. Clearly, Jesus doesn't want us to keep the little commandments in Scripture and miss the big stuff, but neither does he allow us to overlook the smallest parts so long as we get the big picture right. He expects obedience to the spirit of the law and to the letter. Our Messiah sees himself as an expositor of Scripture, but never a corrector of Scripture. He fulfills it, but never falsifies it. He turns away wrong interpretations of Scripture, but insists there is nothing wrong with Scripture, down to the crossing of t's and dotting of i's.

Historical History

Our third text on Jesus's view of the Bible is Matthew 12:38–42:

> Then some of the scribes and Pharisees answered him, saying, "Teacher, we wish to see a sign from you." But he answered them, "An evil and adulterous generation seeks for a sign, but no sign will be given to it except the sign of the prophet Jonah. For just as Jonah was three days and three nights in the belly of the great fish, so will the Son of Man be three days and three nights in the heart of the earth. The men of Nineveh will rise up at the judgment with this generation and condemn it, for they repented at the preaching of Jonah, and behold, something greater than Jonah is here. The queen of the South will rise up at the judgment with this generation and condemn it, for she came from the ends of the earth

to hear the wisdom of Solomon, and behold, something
greater than Solomon is here."

This story is but one example of how Jesus consistently
treats biblical history as a straightforward record of facts. If
any Old Testament reference can be challenged, it is this one
about Jonah. And yet, Jesus speaks confidently about Jonah
in the belly of the great fish, as if he and all his hearers had
no reservations about the historical accuracy of the story.

To be sure, some scholars, even those with a high view of
Scripture, question whether we are meant to take the story
of Jonah literally. After all, the narrative is not from an
obviously historical book like Kings or Chronicles or Exodus.
Jesus could be referencing Jonah as we might reference a
well-known piece of literature. Maybe Jesus meant nothing
more by "just as Jonah" than we would by saying, "just as
the men of Gondor" or "just as Luke and Obi-Wan." Perhaps
Jonah is a fable, and we were never meant to read it is as
history.

This explanation sounds plausible, except that it doesn't
work given the rest of Jesus's speech. If Jonah is only a literary reference, it's curious that in the same breath Jesus men-
tions the Queen of Sheba, clearly a known historical figure.
More critically, it's hard to justify Jesus's language about
the men of Nineveh rising up to judge Capernaum on the
last day if most or all of the Jonah story is not to be taken
literally. It would be like making that literary allusion to the
men of Gondor and then issuing a very serious warning to
your audience that the orcs of Mordor will rise up to judge
and condemn them. It doesn't make a lot of sense. As T. T.
Perowne put it, commenting on the very real danger Jesus

considered his hearers to be in, "And yet we are to suppose him to say that imaginary persons who at the imaginary preaching of an imaginary prophet repented in imagination, shall rise up in that day and condemn the actual impenitence of those his actual hearers?"[3] Quite the contrary. In the Gospels we see Jesus reference Abel, Noah, Abraham, Sodom and Gomorrah, Isaac and Jacob, manna in the wilderness, the serpent in the wilderness, Moses as the lawgiver, David and Solomon, the Queen of Sheba, Elijah and Elisha, the widow of Zarephath, Naaman, Zechariah, and even Jonah, never questioning a single event, a single miracle, or a single historical claim. Jesus clearly believed in the historicity of biblical history.

Rather than finding ways to "rescue" Jesus from his confidence in history as Scripture presents it, we should be prepared to accept that if Jesus is right in how he handles the Bible, then boatloads of higher biblical criticism must be wrong. For the past 150 years or so, many modern scholars have argued that the Old Testament is far from what it seems. The first five books of the Bible were not written by Moses (and later edited in a few places), but are instead the product of an elaborate combination of different sources, some of which are a thousand years later than Moses. Isaiah was not written by Isaiah, but by two or three different "Isaiahs" whose remarkable prophetic predictions actually took place before they ever wrote about them. Most dramatically, if liberal scholars are right, the church misread Israel's history for almost two millennia. Israel's story is not about centuries of struggle to be faithful to the one true God and

---

[3] Quoted in John Wenham, *Christ and the Bible*, 3rd ed. (Eugene, OR: Wipf & Stock, 2009), 20.

obey his law. What actually took place was an evolution-
ary development whereby Israel moved from animism to
polytheism to henotheism (worshiping one God in particular, though recognizing the existence of many) to monotheism to the triumph of priestly legalism. Books that claim to
date from the exodus are later than Ezekiel. First Samuel,
which was thought to be written after the giving of the law,
actually describes Israel's life *before* the law. And the Pentateuch, instead of being the foundation for Israel's life and
religion, came together only after Israel's glory days were
far behind her.[4]

This is part and parcel of what seems plain to so much
modern scholarship, but it isn't even remotely connected to
anything we see from Jesus in the way he handled the Old
Testament. Jesus believed that Israel, during its long history, was under the tutelage of Yahweh; that Moses gave
them a national covenant to live by; that the Pentateuch
came at the beginning of Israel's history, not the end; and
that the prophets rebuked and refined Israel for their failure
to follow God's commandments given at Sinai. And yet, if
the revisionist history of modern critics is correct, Jesus was
monumentally mistaken in believing all this. "He did not de-
tect the strands of animism in Israel's early history," Macleod
writes. "He did not realize that Leviticus was a betrayal of
ethical monotheism. He was blind to the double narratives
that prove composite authorship. He was totally unaware
of the contradictions that demonstrate that Moses did not
write Deuteronomy." Jesus was, in other words, "taken in

---

[4] This paragraph summarizes many of the points made by Donald Macleod, "Jesus and Scripture," 91.

by a national myth no more plausible than that of Romulus and Remus."[5]

Isn't it more plausible to think Jesus knew Jewish history better than German critics almost two thousand years later? Isn't it safer to side with Jesus and adopt his supremely high view of inspiration and his commonsense understanding of biblical history and chronology? We are sometimes told that the final authority for us as Christians should be Christ, and not the Scriptures. It is suggested that Christ would have us accept only the portions of Scripture that comport with his life and teaching; that certain aspects of biblical history, chronology, and cosmology need not bother us because Christ would not have us be bothered by them. The idea put forward by many liberal Christians and by not a few self-proclaimed evangelicals is that we are to worship Christ and not the Scriptures; we must let Christ stand apart from Scripture and above it. "But who is this Christ, the Judge of Scripture?" Packer asks. "Not the Christ of the New Testament and of history. That Christ does not judge Scripture; He obeys it and fulfills it. By word and deed He endorses the authority of the whole of it."[6]

Those with a high view of Scripture are often charged with idolatry for so deeply reverencing the word of God. But the accusation is laid at the wrong feet. "A Christ who permits His followers to set Him up as the Judge of Scripture, One by whom its authority must be confirmed before it becomes binding and by whose adverse sentence it is in places annulled, is a Christ of human imagination, made in the theologian's own image, One whose attitude to Scripture is

---

[5] Ibid., 92.
[6] J. I. Packer, *"Fundamentalism" and the Word of God* (Grand Rapids, MI: Eerdmans, 1958), 61.

the opposite of that of the Christ of history. If the construction of such a Christ is not a breach of the second commandment, it is hard to see what is."[7] Jesus may have seen himself as the focal point of Scripture, but never as a judge of it. The only Jesus who stands above Scripture is the Jesus of our own invention.

The Creator Said

Our final passage for understanding Jesus's doctrine of Scripture is found in Matthew 19. In giving his reply to the Pharisees' question about divorce, Jesus harkens back to Genesis:

> Have you not read that he who created them from the beginning made them male and female, and said, "Therefore a man shall leave his father and his mother and hold fast to his wife, and the two shall become one flesh"? (Matt. 19:4–5)

These verses are so familiar that many of us have missed the amazing statement Jesus makes here about the authorship of Scripture. If you go to Genesis 2:24, you'll find the line Jesus quotes about a man leaving his father and mother, cleaving to his wife, and becoming one flesh. But these words are not attributed to any particular speaker. They're just a part of the narration of the text. But now look at what Jesus says. Genesis 2:24 is not only a line from Scripture; it is a statement said by the one "who created them from the beginning." The implication could not be any plainer: for Jesus, what Scripture says, God says. This is the essence of Jesus's

---

[7] Ibid., 61–62.

doctrine of Scripture and the foundation for any right understanding of the Bible.

And it won't do to argue that Jesus was simply borrowing the assumptions of his audience to win a hearing. In many other areas—in everything from their nationalistic conceptions of a Messiah, to the traditions of the Pharisees, to their treatment of Gentiles and women—Jesus showed himself utterly unconcerned with conforming to the sensitivity of his hearers. But while he wasn't shy about correcting their erroneous *interpretations* of Scripture, there is no indication that Jesus ever thought his fellow Jews to have too high a view of Scripture. And if they had been wrong on such an essential matter, he would not have gone along with the flow. He would have corrected their beliefs about the Bible just as he chastised them for other "doctrines of men."

Jesus has no problem referencing human authors of Scripture like Moses, Isaiah, David, and Daniel. But they stand in the background. They are the sub-authors working beneath the principal author of Scripture, namely, God himself. So Jesus can quote from Psalm 110, saying, "David himself, in the Holy Spirit, declared" (Mark 12:36), just as Paul in Romans 9:17 and Galatians 3:8 can use "Scripture" as the subject where God is the Old Testament speaker. Holy Spirit, God, Scripture—they are not three different speakers with three different ranks. They refer to the same divine author with the same divine authority. Which is why Jesus can talk down the Devil by saying "it is written," and why he can claim, without any hint of controversy or hyperbole, that the Creator of the universe wrote Genesis. For Jesus, Scripture is powerful, decisive, and authoritative because it is nothing less than the voice of God.

The Way of the Master Is the Way of the Word

Jesus held Scripture in the highest possible esteem. He knew his Bible intimately and loved it deeply. He often spoke with the language of Scripture. He easily alluded to Scripture. And in his moments of greatest trial and weakness—like being tempted by the Devil or being killed on a cross—he quoted Scripture.

His mission was to fulfill Scripture, and his teaching always upheld Scripture. He never disrespected, never disregarded, never disagreed with a single text of Scripture. He affirmed every bit of law, prophecy, narrative, and poetry. He never for a moment accepted the legitimacy of anyone anywhere violating, ignoring, refining, or rejecting Scripture.

Jesus believed in the inspiration of Scripture—all of it. He accepted the chronology, the miracles, and the authorial ascriptions as giving the straightforward facts of history. He believed in keeping the spirit of the law without ever minimizing the letter of the law. He affirmed the human authorship of Scripture while at the same time bearing witness to the ultimate divine authorship of the Scriptures. He treated the Bible as a necessary word, a sufficient word, a clear word, and the final word. It was never acceptable in his mind to contradict Scripture or stand above Scripture.

He believed the Bible was all true, all edifying, all important, and all about him. He believed absolutely that the Bible was from God and was absolutely free from error. What Scripture says, God says; and what God said was recorded infallibly in Scripture.

This, then, can be the only acceptable answer to the question posed at the beginning of this chapter about Jesus's doctrine of Scripture: it is impossible to revere the Scriptures more deeply or affirm them more completely than Jesus did. Jesus submitted his will to the Scriptures, committed his brain to studying the Scriptures, and humbled his heart to obey the Scriptures. The Lord Jesus, God's Son and our Savior, believed his Bible was the word of God down to the sentences, to the phrases, to the words, to the smallest letter, to the tiniest specks—and that nothing in all those specks and in all those books in his Holy Bible could ever be broken.

8

Stick With the Scriptures

But as for you, continue in what you have learned and have firmly believed, knowing from whom you learned it and how from childhood you have been acquainted with the sacred writings, which are able to make you wise for salvation through faith in Christ Jesus. All Scripture is breathed out by God and profitable for teaching, for reproof, for correction, and for training in righteousness, that the man of God may be complete, equipped for every good work.

2 TIMOTHY 3:14–17

Picking up a book on the doctrine of Scripture, you might have figured this would be the first chapter, not the last. After all, 2 Timothy 3:16 is the most famous verse about the Bible in the whole Bible. In one sense, nothing more needs to be said about Scripture once we know that all of it has been breathed out by God. This is the very definition of inspiration: everything in the Bible comes from the mouth of God. Sufficiency, clarity, authority, and necessity—they must all be true if 2 Timothy 3:16 is true, and they would all be false if 2 Timothy 3:16 were a lie. There is no more important verse for developing a proper understanding of Scripture.

And yet, I end here. I began with Psalm 119 and finish with 2 Timothy 3, just the opposite of what you might expect.

I do so for two reasons: First, so you can see that, as

significant as this passage might be for our doctrine of Scripture, it says nothing different from dozens of other verses. With everything else we've already seen about the Bible from the Bible, it should come as no surprise to see (again) this affirmation that what Scripture says, God says. Every expression of the psalmist's delight in the word of God, desire for the word of God, and dependence on the word of God presupposes that every word of the word of God, whether spoken or written, is breathed out by God himself. If the view of inspiration taught in 2 Timothy 3:16 were not already assumed, Psalm 119 would be tantamount to idolatry.

Second, we end with this passage because of its emphasis on continuing (2 Tim. 3:14). While I'd be thrilled to find out that many seekers were reading this book, I think it's safe to assume that if you've made it this far, you are probably a Christian. Most of you have read the Bible before. That's why you are interested in knowing what to believe about the Bible. You've already been taught the Scriptures, at least in part. And the fact that you are reading this book suggests you already have a devotion to the Bible or are open to growing in your devotion to the Bible. So the most appropriate exhortation at the close of this book may be the one in verse 14: Continue. Don't forget what you know and have already learned. Don't lose sight of who you are. Stay on track. Keep on going.

At the beginning of verse 14, Paul introduces a contrast. He's thinking, on the one hand, of those who persecute him (v. 11). He's thinking of evil people and imposters who go on from bad to worse (v. 13). He's probably thinking of men like Demas, who left him (4:10), and men like Alexander, who did him great harm (4:14). And then he says, "But as for you, . . ." (3:14). That's the other hand; that's the contrast. Paul is warning Timothy not to be like these deceivers and deserters. He says, "Look, you have been brought up in the gospel—rooted, grounded, established. The challenge for you now is to keep growing; keep moving in the same direction; keep firm in the same faith."

And this means, more than anything else, that Timothy must stay close to the word of God. The command to continue in the gospel is, for Timothy just as for all of us, an exhortation to keep going with and keep growing in the sacred writings (v. 15). "Stay on target"—that was good advice as Luke Skywalker approached the Death Star, and it's good advice for every Christian. Don't go wobbly. Don't wander from the way. That's the message of 2 Timothy 3:14–17. We will be tempted and tried. We will get tired. We will know many pressures. We will be persecuted if we desire to live a godly life in Christ Jesus (v. 12). But this is God's never-changing instruction to us: stick with the Scriptures, and steady as she goes.

Consider Your History

Thankfully, Paul doesn't stop with this simple command to continue; he gives reasons. We see in 2 Timothy 3:14–17 four reasons we should stick with the Scriptures: our history, Scripture's ability, Scripture's originality, and Scripture's practicality. We'll start with Paul's urging that we consider our own history.

I realize this first point is not equally applicable to every Christian. Many believers have only recently come to Christ. Millions have no Christian history to consider at all. But it still is the case—and, I would argue, by God's design always will be the case—that the most natural way Christian commitment is spread is through the family. And even when our natural family played no role in our coming to faith, we all have some person in our history who was God's chosen means of saving grace. So in one way or another, Paul's exhortation to Timothy is God's exhortation to us. Remember who led you to faith. Remember who told you the gospel. Remember who first taught you the Bible.

For Timothy, this meant Paul to some extent (2:2), and more significantly, his grandmother Lois and his mother Eunice (1:5; 3:14–15). Paul is urging this young pastor to stick with the Bible and stick with the one true gospel because he learned about them from his grammy and from his momma. We don't often reason this way, but we should. Before chucking the faith you were taught as a child, think about those from whom you learned it. I went to a middle-of-the-road Christian college where the religion professors were often liberal. I saw many of my classmates have their faith deconstructed and never built up again in a healthy way. When people ask me why I didn't go down the same path, the best answer I have—besides noting the grace of God—is that I trusted my parents and my upbringing more than my professors. I had doubts as a college student. There were new questions I didn't know how to answer. But what kept me anchored was confidence in what I had learned as a child and in those from whom I had learned it.

Obviously, not everyone is blessed to grow up with good parents and good churches. But this doesn't make Paul's command to Timothy any less appropriate for those of us who did. Think of your Sunday school teachers. Think of your youth group leaders. Think of your pastors. Think of your dad. Think of your grandparents. Think of your mom. Did they not have your best interests at heart? Did they not love you? Were they imposters? Were they wrong in everything they stood for? Is it reasonable for you to conclude that those who came before you, those who taught you to trust the Bible, those who have more experience and probably more wisdom than you—that suddenly they are benighted morons? Are they deserving of your cynicism, rejection, or scorn?

Parents and pastors aren't perfect, not even the really good ones. Paul is not saying our mentors must be followed at all costs. But here's the point, and it's very appropriate for teens and twentysomethings who like to question every authority except their own: before you leave behind what you used to believe about the Bible, consider who taught you to believe what you used to believe about the Bible.

I remember on a conference panel someone asking John Piper, "Why did you conclude inerrancy is true?" The first thing out of his mouth surprised everyone: "Because my momma told me it's true." Yet that wasn't a throwaway line or a glib remark crafted for effect. Piper was capturing something deeply true in many of our lives, and deeply biblical. It's not necessarily a sign of growth to move past the faith of your childhood, and not necessarily a weakness to believe the same thing throughout your whole life. What an inestimable privilege to be acquainted from childhood with the sacred writings. The ultimate reason for Timothy to stick with the Scripture goes far beyond Lois and Eunice. But at their feet is where he first learned to trust the word of God. Which is no small thing, and not to be tossed aside for anything in the world.

Consider Scripture's Ability

The word of God is able to do many things—everything, really. God created by the word. Abraham was called by the word. The people were gathered as a nation at Sinai by the word. Their deliverance from Babylon was made firm by the word. Lazarus was raised by the word. The apostolic church was called into existence by the word. Throughout redemptive history we see God creating, cursing, calling, converting, gathering, blessing, equipping, threatening, and promising by his word. And in our personal history, we see the power of God's word most clearly in its ability to save us (2 Tim. 3:15).

Scripture doesn't tell us everything we may want to know about everything. But it tells us everything we need to know about the most important things. It gives us something the Internet, with all its terabytes of information, never could: wisdom. The purpose of Holy Scripture is not ultimately to make you smart, or make you relevant, or make you rich, or get you a job, or get you married, or take all your problems away, or tell you where to live. The aim is that you might be wise enough to put your faith in Christ and be saved.

Nothing else in all the world has this ability. The word of the president is important. The word of your parents is to be honored. The word of your spouse is to be treasured. But only the word of God can save. Only in Scripture do we encounter the fullness of God's self-disclosure. Only in Scripture do we find the good news of the forgiveness of sins. Only in Scripture can we be led to believe in Jesus Christ and, by believing, have life in his name. Don't think you have nothing important to say in the world. Don't worry whether you have anything helpful to share with hurting and needy people. Don't despair that there is no transforming power in your life. Keep going in the gospel, and keep growing in the Scriptures. They are more than able.

Consider Scripture's Originality

By "originality" I'm not referring to the creativity or artistry of Scripture. I'm using the word more literally to refer to the origin of Scripture: where it came from, and who is responsible for it. Second Timothy 3:16 gives the justly famous answer: "All Scripture is *breathed out* by God." Over the last century or so, some scholars have tried to argue that Scripture is "inspired" in the sense that it is an inspiring book and can inspire us. But B. B. Warfield comprehensively demolished this new interpretation more than a hundred years ago, concluding after meticulous scholarship that *theopneustos* (the Greek word translated "breathed out by God" in the ESV) is "primarily expressive of the *origination* of Scripture, not of its nature and much less of its effects."[1] As Warfield says elsewhere, "The Biblical writers do not conceive of the Scriptures as a human product breathed into by the Divine Spirit, and thus heightened in its qualities or endowed with new qualities; but as a Divine product produced through the instrumentality of men."[2] The inspiration of Scripture is a past established fact, not a future hoped-for occurrence. Scripture is not just inspiring, but inspired; not just breathed, but breathed out. As the verbal expression of

---

[1] Benjamin B. Warfield, *The Inspiration and Authority of the Bible* (Phillipsburg, NJ: Presbyterian & Reformed, 1948), 296.
[2] Ibid., 153.

Christ's lordship, Scripture carries all the weight of divine authority because it comes entirely from divine origination.

And this is true for *all* Scripture. Every book, every chapter, every line, every word—all of it is breathed out by God. Not just the obviously theological parts. Not just the memorable stuff. Not just the parts that resonate with us. All of it—history, chronology, philosophy—every truth the Bible affirms ought to be taken as God's truth. Every word in the Bible is in there because God wanted it there. And therefore, we should listen to the Bible and stick with the Bible and submit ourselves to the teaching of the Bible because it is God's Bible—both the sacred writings of the Old Testament, which Paul first of all had in mind, and the inspired writings for the new covenant church, which Paul understood himself to be issuing (1 Thess. 2:13) and Peter understood to be in the process of being written down (2 Pet. 3:16).

Just as crucially, if all Scripture is breathed out by God, then there is a unity to be found across the pages of the Bible. Without minimizing the differences of genre and human authorship, we should nevertheless approach the Bible expecting theological distinctives and apparent discrepancies to be fully reconcilable.

The unity of Scripture also means we should be rid, once and for all, of this "red letter" nonsense, as if the words of Jesus are the really important verses in Scripture and carry more authority and are somehow more directly divine than other verses. An evangelical understanding of inspiration does not allow us to prize instructions in the gospel more than instructions elsewhere in Scripture. If we read about homosexuality from the pen of Paul in Romans, it has no less weight or relevance than if we read it from the lips of Jesus in Matthew. All Scripture is breathed out by God, not just the parts spoken by Jesus.

God's gracious self-disclosure comes to us through the Word made flesh and by the inscripturated word of God. These two modes of revelation reveal to us one God, one truth, one way, and one coherent set of promises, threats, and commands to live by. We must not seek to know the Word who is divine apart from the divine words of the Bible, and we ought not read the words of the Bible without an eye to the Word incarnate. When it comes to seeing God and his truth in Christ and in Holy Scripture, one is not more reliable, more trustworthy, or more relevant than the other. Scripture, because it is the breathed-out word of God, possesses the same authority as the God-man Jesus Christ. Submission to the Scriptures is submission to God. Rebellion against the Scriptures is rebellion against God. The Bible can no more fail, falter, or err, than God himself can fail, falter, or err.

This high view of Scripture as the inerrant, God-breathed word of God has been the position of Christians from the beginning. Clement of Rome (30–100) described "the Sacred Scriptures" as "the true utterance of the Holy Spirit" and wrote that "in them there hath not been written anything that is unrighteous or counterfeit." Irenaeus (120–202) claimed that the biblical writers "were filled with perfect knowledge on every subject" and were "incapable of a false statement." According to Origen (185–254), "the sacred volumes are fully inspired by the Holy Spirit, and there is no passage either in the Law or the Gospel, or the writings of an Apostle, which does not proceed from the inspired source of Divine Truth." Augustine (354–430) explained in a letter to Jerome, "I have learnt to ascribe to those Books which are of the Canonical rank, and only to them, such reverence and honour, that I firmly believe that no single error due to the author is found in any of them." Jerome (393–c. 457) declared the Scriptures to be "the most pure fount. . . . written and edited by the Holy Spirit."[3] Aquinas (1225–1274) argued, "The Author of Holy Scripture is God."[4] Calvin (1509–1564) claimed that if we follow the Scriptures we will be "safe from the danger of erring." We ought to embrace "without finding fault, whatever is taught in Sacred Scripture." We "owe to the Scripture the same reverence which we owe to God." In Scripture, God "opens his own most hallowed lips," and the apostles were "sure and genuine scribes of the Holy Spirit."[5] It would not be hard to continue to multiply quotations like this from Calvin, and his view of inspiration was far from novel.

Until fairly recently, Christians of every tradition have assumed the complete trustworthiness and comprehensive truthfulness of Scripture. Holding to the highest view of inspiration—as originated with God himself—was not the invention of any tradition, theologian, or school. It was simply part of what it meant to be a Christian.

Consider Scripture's Practicality

The final rationale Paul gives for sticking with the Scriptures is their practicality. This may seem like a lame reason for continuing with the word of God, especially after looking at all this *theopneustos* business. But for Paul, Scripture's

---

[3] These citations can be found in Carl F. H. Henry, *God, Revelation, and Authority*, 6 vols. (Wheaton, IL: Crossway, 1999), 4:370–372.
[4] *Summa Theologica* I.i.10, in *Introduction to St. Thomas Aquinas*, ed. Anton C. Pegis (New York: Modern Library, 1965).
[5] These five quotations come from, respectively, *Commentary on Matthew* 22:29; *Institutes* 1.18.4; *Institutes* 1.6.1 (cf. 1.8.5); *Institutes* 2.12.1 (see also 1.8.5; 3.22.8; 3.23.5; *Commentary on 1 Peter* 1:25); *Institutes* 4.8.9.

practicality is the conclusion of his whole argument. It's the payoff and the point of all this grand theology.

Scripture is profitable for teaching. It tells us who God is and what he demands. It tells us who we are, why we are here, where we are from, and where we are going. It tells us about love and marriage. It tells us about life before our life and about life after death. Most of all, it tells us about sin and forgiveness, about Christ and the cross, about how we are lost and how to be found. And because Scripture says what God says, we can completely trust everything Scripture says about all of this.

Scripture is profitable for reproof and correction. It convicts and consoles. It cuts and comforts. It stops us short when we mess up and sets us back on the right path. God gave us the Bible because he loves us enough to tell us what he thinks and to tell us how to live.

Scripture is profitable for training in righteousness. No one succeeds at the highest level in sports without working out. No one makes it in music without lots of practice. No one excels in scholarship without years of study. And no one makes it far in the school of holiness without hours and days and years in the word. You and I simply will not mature as quickly, minister as effectively, or live as gloriously without immersing ourselves in the Scriptures.

We need the Bible if we are to be competent Christians. The Bible will build us up so that we can endure suffering. It will give us discernment for difficult choices. It will make us strong enough to be patient with others and patient enough to respond with kindness when others hurt us. The Bible will get us up to bring meals to new moms and pray for people on their hospital beds. The Bible equips us to be truth lovers and truth tellers. It sends us out to care for the poor and welcome the stranger. There is no limit to what the Bible can do for us, to us, and through us. We can never outgrow the Bible, because it always means to make us grow. The Bible is only impractical for the immature, and only irrelevant for the fools who believe that most everything is new under the sun.

It Is a Serious Thing

I began this book with a long poem—with a love poem about singing, speaking, studying, storing up, obeying, praising, and praying the word of God. I started with the application, in hope that by the end, the joy and confidence in the psalmist's heart would be exploding out of ours. With everything we now know about the Bible, from the Bible, we should have our hearts tuned for praise and our minds girded for action.

And we should be ready to continue—to continue in the truth of God's word, to continue in the reading and hearing of God's word, and to continue believing everything affirmed in God's word. In a world that prizes the new, the progressive, and the evolved, we need to be reminded that Jesus Christ is the same yesterday, today, and forever (Heb. 13:8). And since he remains the same, so does his truth. Which means sometimes consistency is the better part of valor. Charles Hodge, the great Princeton theologian from the nineteenth century, has been ridiculed for his boast that a new idea never originated at Princeton Seminary. But to paint this statement with darkest hues is, as one of Hodge's recent biographers points out, to devalue Hodge's greatest gift: his utter consistency of conviction. "Taken in its original context, Hodge's comment

does capture the very essence of the man. He was not interested in theological innovation because he believed it impossible to improve on orthodox belief."[6] Hodge was not looking
for new ideas about God, because he believed the truth had
already been revealed. And he committed his life to the explanation and defense of the Scriptures because he believed, as
Jesus did, that above all else, the most fundamental thing we
can say about God's word—amid a hundred things we can and
should say—is that God's word is truth (John 17:17).

John Newton, the slave trader turned pastor and hymn
writer, tells the story of visiting a simple woman who died
at a young age from "a lingering consumption." She was a
"sober, prudent person, of plain sense, could read her Bible,
but had read little besides." Newton supposed she had never
traveled more than twelve miles from home. A few days before her death, Newton prayed with her and "thanked the
Lord that he gave her now to see that she had not followed
cunningly-devised fables." At this last remark the woman repeated Newton's words and said, "No, not cunningly-devised
fables; these are realities indeed." Then she fixed her eyes
upon Newton, reminding him of his weighty vocation and the
seriousness of truth:

> Sir, you are highly favored in being called to preach the
> gospel. I have often heard you with pleasure; but give me
> leave to tell you, that I now see all you have said, or can
> say, is comparatively but little. Nor, till you come into
> my situation, and have death and eternity in full view,
> will it be possible for you to conceive the vast weight and
> importance of the truths you declare.

---

[6] Paul C. Gutjahr, *Charles Hodge: The Guardian of American Orthodoxy* (Oxford: Oxford University Press, 2011), 363.

Reflecting on the woman's final days, Newton recalled that "in all she spoke there was a dignity, weight, and evidence, which I suppose few professors of divinity, when lecturing from the chair, have at any time equaled." He found in her testimony— as he often did in visiting the sick and dying—"corroborating evidence" for the grand truths of the gospel spoken by God in his word. "Oh! Sir," the young woman exclaimed, "it is a serious thing to die; no words can express what is needful to support the soul in the solemnity of a dying hour."[7]

No words can express what is needful in our dying hour. But there *are* words to sustain us in that moment, and in every moment from this hour until that. They are the words of truth, the words of life, the never-failing, never-falling, Christ-exalting, Spirit-inspired, God-breathed words of Holy Scripture. Sticking with the Scriptures may seem like a light thing now, but we will feel the weight of it someday. There will come a time when it will be shown whether our lives were founded upon trivialities or realities.

So let us not weaken in our commitment to our unbreakable Bible. Let us not wander from this divinely exhaled truth. Let us not waver in our delight and desire. God has spoken, and through that revelation he still speaks. Ultimately we can believe the Bible because we believe in the power and wisdom and goodness and truthfulness of the God whose authority and veracity cannot be separated from the Bible. We trust the Bible because it is God's Bible. And God being God, we have every reason to take him at his word.

---

[7] This story, including these quotations, can be found in *Letters of John Newton* (Edinburgh: Banner of Truth, 2007 [1869]), 100–101.

Appendix

Thirty of the Best Books
on the Good Book

This annotated bibliography is not meant to be exhaustive. It's simply a list of the thirty books I have found most helpful in developing and defending a biblical doctrine of Scripture. In order to highlight the most obtainable resources for a general audience, I've limited myself to books (i.e., no journal articles, no encyclopedia entries) and have tried to stick with those that are somewhat easily accessible. This has skewed the list toward more recent books. Each volume is labeled "Beginner," "Intermediate," or "Advanced," so that you can have some idea of which book is right for you.

Apologetic Concerns

Blomberg, Craig. *The Historical Reliability of the Gospels* (IVP Academic, 2007). Covers miracles, apparent contradictions, the synoptic problem, and other areas related to the trustworthiness of the four Gospels. (Intermediate)

Bruce, F. F. *The New Testament Documents: Are They Reliable?* (Eerdmans, 2003 [1960]). Similar to Blomberg's volume, but shorter, simpler, and more focused on the documents themselves. (Beginner)

Jones, Timothy Paul. *Misquoting Truth: A Guide to the Fallacies of Bart Ehrman's "Misquoting Jesus"* (InterVarsity Press, 2007). An excellent response to Ehrman's "much ado about nothing" book on textual criticism. (Beginner)

Kaiser, Walter. *The Old Testament Documents: Are They Reliable and Relevant?* (IVP Academic, 2001). Looks at the same sorts of issues as its New Testament counterpart: canon, history, archaeology, and textual transmission. (Intermediate)

Kruger, Michael J. *Canon Revisited: Establishing the Origins and Authority of the New Testament Books* (Crossway, 2012). A terrific blend of history and theology put to good use in explaining the development of our self-authenticating canon. (Advanced)

Classics

Bavinck, Herman. *Reformed Dogmatics, Volume One: Prolegomena* (Baker Academic, 2003 [1906]), pages 283–494. You won't find a better two hundred pages on the doctrine of Scripture from a Reformed perspective—brilliant, broad, and biblical. (Advanced)

Calvin, John. *Institutes of the Christian Religion* (Westminster John Knox, 1960 [1559]), book 1, chapters 1–10. More devotional and easier to understand than you might think. (Intermediate)

Lillback, Peter A., and Richard B. Gaffin Jr. *Thy Word Is Still Truth: Essential Writings on the Doctrine of Scripture from the Reformation to Today* (Presbyterian & Reformed, 2013). A remarkable collection of the most important statements on Scripture from those in the Reformed confessional tradition, especially in the line of Old Princeton. (Advanced)

Machen, J. Gresham. *Christianity and Liberalism* (Eerdmans, 2009 [1923]). Still the best antidote to the allure of theological modernism. (Beginner)

Turretin, Francis. *Institutes of Elenctic Theology, Volume One* (Presbyterian & Reformed, 1997 [1679]), pages 55–167. Orderly in presentation and meticulous in substance; an overlooked classic. (Advanced)

Warfield, Benjamin B. *The Inspiration and Authority of the Bible* (Presbyterian & Reformed, 1948). A collection of Warfield's articles from the end of the nineteenth and beginning of the twentieth centuries; perhaps the most important influential book written on the doctrine of Scripture in the last 150 years. (Advanced)

General Works on the Doctrine of Scripture

Carson, D. A. *Collected Writings on Scripture* (Crossway, 2010). No one writing on the doctrine of Scripture today writes more trenchantly and perceptively than Carson. (Intermediate)

Carson, D. A., and John D. Woodbridge, eds. *Hermeneutics, Authority, and Canon* (Baker, 1995). A very worthwhile collection of essays from the likes of Vanhoozer, Silva, Blomberg, and Moo. (Intermediate)

———. *Scripture and Truth* (Baker, 1992). The precursor to the volume above; includes fine essays from Grudem, Godfrey, Nicole, and Packer. (Intermediate)

Frame, John. *The Doctrine of the Word of God* (Presbyterian & Reformed, 2010). Despite a surprisingly low view of preaching and seventeen appendices, this may be the best contemporary single volume work on the subject. (Beginner)

Grudem, Wayne A. "Part 1: The Doctrine of the Word of God." Pages 45–138 in *Systematic Theology: An Introduction to Biblical Doctrine* (Zondervan, 1994). Exceptionally clear, well organized, and grounded in Scripture. (Beginner)

Helm, Paul, and Carl Trueman, eds. *The Trustworthiness of God: Perspectives on the Nature of Scripture* (Eerdmans, 2002). Some chapters are better than others; the ones by Macleod, Trueman, Ward, and Helm are particularly strong. (Intermediate)

Henry, Carl F. H. *God, Revelation, and Authority*, 6 vols. (Crossway, 1999). The most comprehensive defense of an evangelical doctrine of Scripture; dense, exhaustive, and magisterial. (Advanced)

Nichols, Stephen J., and Eric T. Brandt. *Ancient Word, Changing Worlds: The Doctrine of Scripture in a Modern Age* (Crossway, 2009). A narrative and documentary history of the battle for the Bible in the last hundred-plus years. (Beginner)

Packer, J. I. *"Fundamentalism" and the Word of God* (Eerdmans, 1958). Written for the controversies of another time and place, but still remarkably relevant; if you are going to read just one book on the doctrine of Scripture, read this one. (Intermediate)

————. *Truth and Power* (Harold Shaw, 1996). Great sections on preaching and the importance of the term "inerrancy." (Beginner)

Thompson, Mark D. *A Clear and Present Word: The Clarity of Scripture* (InterVarsity Press, 2006). The best short volume on perspicuity; particular attention is given to the theology of Martin Luther. (Intermediate)

Ward, Timothy. *Words of Life: Scripture as the Living and Active Word of God* (IVP Academic, 2009). An excellent summary of classic Reformation theology, building on Calvin, Turretin, Bavinck, and Warfield; strong Trinitarian focus; affirms inerrancy but downplays its importance. (Intermediate)

Wenham, John. *Christ and the Bible*, 3rd ed. (Wipf & Stock, 2009). One of the best book-length examinations of how Jesus views the Scriptures. (Intermediate)

Woodbridge, John D. *Biblical Authority: A Critique of the Rogers / McKim Proposal* (Zondervan, 1982). Demolished the Rogers/McKim proposal, which argued that inerrancy is an aberration in the history of the church and was not the doctrine of the Reformers. (Intermediate)

How to Study and Interpret the Bible

Plummer, Robert. *40 Questions about Interpreting the Bible* (Kregel Academic, 2010). A wonderful tool for any discipleship class and for any disciple. (Beginner)

Sproul, R. C. *Knowing Scripture* (InterVarsity Press, 2009). Originally published in 1977, this updated edition (like the Plummer volume) looks at principles for interpretation and gives many practical suggestions for studying the Bible. (Beginner)

Inerrancy

Beale, G. K. *The Erosion of Inerrancy in Evangelicalism: Responding to New Challenges to Biblical Authority* (Crossway, 2008). A necessary and vigorous defense of inerrancy in the wake of Peter Enns's book *Incarnation and Inspiration*. (Advanced)

Geisler, Norman L., ed. *Inerrancy* (Zondervan, 1980). An important collection of essays from an earlier day; Feinberg's chapter on the meaning of inerrancy is especially valuable. (Intermediate)

Poythress, Vern Sheridan. *Inerrancy and Worldview* (Crossway, 2012). Demonstrates convincingly that inerrancy is a doctrine that matters for all of life. See also the companion volume, *Inerrancy and the Gospels*. (Intermediate)

General Index

inerrancy, 38–40
inspiration, 36, 111–112, 117–118;
    evangelical theory of, 36–37;
    and human instrumentality
    (concursive operation), 36–38
Irenaeus, 119

Jerome, 120
Jesus: as God's full and final act
    of redemption and God's full
    and final revelation of himself,
    50; as a king, 51; as the morn-
    ing star rising in our hearts, 36;
    as a priest, 51; as a prophet, 51;
    resurrection of, 33, 40; transfig-
    uration of, 30, 33–34, 40; as the
    word made flesh, 21; "you have
    heard it was said" statements
    of, 100–101. *See also* Jesus,
    beliefs about the Scriptures;
    Jesus, as the superior and final
    agent of God's redemption and
    revelation
Jesus, beliefs of about the
    Scriptures, 21, 64–65, 95–96,
    109–110; biblical history is a
    straightforward record of facts,
    102–107; God is the author of
    Scripture, 106–107; "Scripture
    cannot be broken," 97–98; there
    is nothing wrong with Scrip-
    ture, down to the crossing of t's
    and dotting of i's, 98–102
Jesus, as the superior and final
    agent of God's redemption and
    revelation: he has become much
    superior to angels, 48; he is the
    creator of all things, 48; he is
    the heir of all things, 47; he is
    the revelation of God, 48; he is
    the sustainer of all things, 48;

he made purification for our
    sins, 48; he sat down, 48

knowledge of God: archetypal
    knowledge, 66; ectypal knowl-
    edge, 66
Kreeft, Peter, 76–77, 78

lex talionis (Latin: law of retalia-
    tion), 100–101
liberal theology, on truth claims,
    77
love poems, 11–15
luo (Greek: to break), 98, 99

Macleod, Donald, 101, 105–106
"My Conversation with God"
    (anonymous), 27–28, 46
myth, 30–32; as the foundation
    of paganism (the Greeks and
    Romans), 32; liberal scholars'
    use of the category of "myth"
    to describe the Bible, 30–31; as
    the opposite of truth in the New
    Testament, 31–32
mythos (Greek: myth), 31–32

neoorthodoxy, 34–35
Newton, John, 123–124

Old Testament: and German
    higher biblical criticism,
    104–106; as "the Law and the
    Prophets," 35
Origen, 119

Packer, J. I., 24, 40, 52, 82,
    106–107
Perowne, T. T., 103–104
phero (Greek: to produce, to
    carry), 37–38

Spirit of God, 88–89; nothing is more sure than the word of God, 40–42; as the "prophetic word," "prophecy of Scripture," and "prophecy," 34, 35; unity of, 118–119; as without error, 38–40. *See also* inerrancy; inspiration; sticking with the Scriptures; word of God, authority of; word of God, clarity of; word of God, necessity of; word of God, sufficiency of

word of God, attributes of. *See* word of God, authority of; word of God, clarity of; word of God, necessity of; word of God, sufficiency of

word of God, authority of, 44, 45, 76–78, 92; and difficulties and apparent discrepancies in the Bible, 81–82

word of God, clarity of, 44, 45, 92; the Catholic objection to, 60; confirmation of throughout the Bible, 63–65; definition of, 58–59; the mystical objection to, 59–60; and the nearness of the word of God, 61–63; the plural-ism objection to, 60–61. *See also* word of God, clarity of, what is at stake with this doctrine

word of God, clarity of, what is at stake with this doctrine: the gift of human freedom, 67–68; the gift of human language, 65–67; what God is like, 68–69; whom God is for, 69–70

word of God, necessity of, 44, 45, 86–87, 88–90, 91, 92

word of God, perfection of. *See* word of God, sufficiency of

word of God, perspicuity of. *See* word of God, clarity of

word of God, sufficiency of, 44, 45–46, 92; and the invitation to us to open our Bibles to hear the voice of God, 55; and Jesus as the superior and final agent of God's redemption and revelation, 46–49; and the keeping of tradition in its place, 52–53; and not adding or subtracting from the word of God, 53–54; and the relevancy of the word of God to all of life, 54–55

Scripture Index

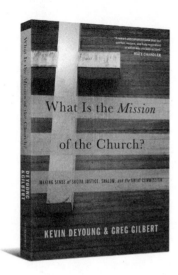

Also Available from
KEVIN DEYOUNG

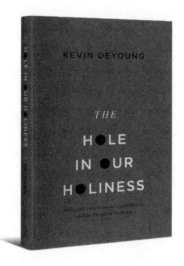